ANGELS
PLAIN & SIMPLE

BELETA GREENAWAY

THE ONLY BOOK YOU'LL EVER NEED

HAMPTON ROADS

Cover design by Jim Warner
Interior design by Kathryn Sky-Peck

Hampton Roads Publishing Company, Inc.
Charlottesville, VA 22906
Distributed by Red Wheel/Weiser, LLC
www.redwheelweiser.com
Sign up for our newsletter and special offers by going to
www.redwheelweiser.com/newsletter/

ISBN: 978-1-57174-755-6

Library of Congress Cataloging-in-Publication Data available upon request
Printed in Canada
MG

10 9 8 7 6 5 4 3 2 1

Contents

Who Are These Beings?

I clearly remember my first impression of angels. It happened when I was a five-year-old little girl. I was dressed in a white gossamer bridesmaid's gown, trimmed with violet blue ribbons. I felt very important as I clutched my small posy of cream and lavender freesia, while I attended my very first wedding ceremony; but as I was so young, I found my attention wandering during the ceremony.

Even at that tender age, I could appreciate the beauty of the church. It was erected in the 15th century and it was located in the sleepy Somerset village in England where I was born. The many stained glass windows sent prisms of light into the congregation as they sang, "All Things Bright And Beautiful." The font was over-large and made of pale stone with strange gothic markings carved into the sides. It was the same font in which I had been christened when I was a baby. Above the transept, a huge wooden arch dominated the interior of the church, and emblazoned over it was a painting of the Christ. Positioned around him were six angels and I stared in amazement at the size and splendor of these images, feeling a prickling sensation travel up my spine. Two of the angels were playing musical instruments, another was holding a spray of six white lilies, and yet another was holding the Scales of Justice. The remaining two, on either side of him, had their heads bowed reverently.

"Who are these beings? Do their wings really work?" I asked myself. And if so, "How could they fly . . . and did Jesus really look like that or perhaps it wasn't Jesus, at all, but God?" The little blonde pageboy next to me, dressed in his white satin suit, jabbed me with his elbow. "Come on, we've got to move on now," he

whispered. Concentrating as only a five-year-old can, I purposely moved forward with the rest of the entourage.

As we left the church, I glanced back for one last look at the wonderful angels in all of their colorful splendor—and then totally forgot about them until I was in my middle twenties.

Numerous books have been written about these wonderful beings and I feel so privileged to be able to add my contribution. As you read this book, you will feel in your heart that you gravitate toward certain chapters, and that some other chapters may not resonate with your truth. Follow your heart, and trust your intuition. It is a fact that we all go at our own pace and that we must all find our own way forward.

For three decades I have worked as a clairvoyant, so some of you might wonder why, of all people, I am writing a book about angels, especially as some religious factions believe that to do the work I do, I must have sold my soul to the devil. Some believe the gift of clairvoyance, seeing into the future, is at odds with what they believe is religious faith. The truth is that we all have the ability to know more about the unseen world, if we decide to travel on that particular pathway. The clairvoyants whom I have met have been special souls who have helped so many. They are what we would call the modern day soothsayers, or spiritual life coaches, who through their readings, can give focus to others in times of hardship and doubt. Sadly for many people, conventional religion does not seem to provide any spiritual hope. In my life, I have met many people who love my work and also many who look down on what I do. It doesn't bother me any more, because I have learned to take life as it comes and I have learned that we cannot please all the people all the time.

On one occasion, I attended a very special wedding and I was seated with ten people at a round table adorned with damask tablecloths and fine crystal. The middle-aged minister, who had just conducted the wedding, looked pointedly at me and for some strange reason asked what I did for a living. Suddenly there was a hushed silence as all eyes turned in my direction. "Oh dear," I thought. "This is going to be difficult."

"I'm a clairvoyant," I said. He looked ruffled and his little bird-like wife, who was sitting next to him, shifted uncomfortably in her seat.

"Umm," he replied pompously. "Are you aware of the serious-ness of what you have just said?"

Slowly I put my knife and fork down on the plate and gave him my full attention. "I am sorry, but I don't quite understand you."

"You do realize that you could be denied entrance to heaven when you pass over?"

My mother had taught me never to argue about politics or religion, but here I was about to go into a full-scale debate. The preacher fixed me with a steely gaze and puffed up his chest in a self-important manner, "I'll pray for your soul, my child."

I got angry, we were here solely to celebrate the wedding of my dearest friend and I knew this so-called man of God was champing at the bit and couldn't wait to force his opinions on me and on to the rest of the guests. This was not why I had come to this happy event, and I felt resentful at being targeted. The others sucked in their breath, all eyes riveted on the tension between us. One of the guests leaned across and touched my arm sympatheti-cally. With grim determination I felt I had to ignore my mother's good advice and stick up for myself as I answered him quietly.

"I do believe in a Divine being. I feel especially guided by angels and I believe they are there in the afterlife. I also believe you are judged on your actions in life and not the particular church that you ascribe to. Being a clairvoyant is no sin. I am not a dreadful person and my gift was given to me by God!"

Suddenly one of the other guests spoke up and agreed with me, and then another. One lady was an aromatherapist, another was a healer, and then a spiritualist came into the debate. The preacher was outnumbered and he looked decidedly uncomfortable. This

must have been the first time in his life that he had been unable to hide behind the authority of his position, and he mumbled under his breath he was obviously the odd one out. Through this experience, I have realized that many of us have moved on and that many of us now have a more tolerant attitude toward other faiths and viewpoints.

In this book I am sharing with you some of the experiences I have encountered with angels in my life. To some, these experiences might seem small and insignificant, but in my heart I know the help and information is real. The skeptics among us would perhaps want more proof, but the angelic realms work in a very subtle way. I have read of fortunate people who have had mind-blowing encounters with them and at times I have really envied those people and longed for the same experiences. Mostly my encounters with angels have been intangible. "Was it my imagination? Did I really dream that? Did I hear that?"

I no longer beat myself up about the whys and wherefores. I trust that any information the angels want to give me will be correct and that it will come at the right time. I say to my readers, if you fervently ask for help and information, you will receive it. If you feel unwell or depressed, ask the angels to rectify this, and you will see an improvement. Once the angels start to work with you, there will come a time when you get to "know" or "feel" them around you. It is just a matter of experimenting. I know they can create miracles and bring great peace of mind and strength to the suffering and the weak. Never think you are too small or insignificant for them to attend you. They love to be of service in any way they can.

So now let us look at some true stories about angels.

Encounters with Angels

1

In the middle of the 1950s, when I was about eleven years old, my sandy-haired stepbrother Robert was then just a toddler. Robert became seriously ill, and I can remember clearly one of his little ears being bright red and sticking out like a trumpet. The doctor was called immediately. Within a few hours, Robert was rushed to Frenchay Neurological Hospital in Bristol, England, with a critical brain tumor. Surgery was scheduled for the next day, but the surgeons feared he only had a 10 percent chance of recovery. My mother, a simple country girl who came from a large family, was inconsolable.

At sunrise the following morning, she was lying in bed after a restless night's sleep. On the quilt a few feet away from her, a small image began to appear. It was a beautiful angel, about ten inches high, gently rocking a baby's crib which had an iridescent glow over it. Staring straight at my mother, the angel wrapped her wings around the crib in a protective gesture, her gaze never leaving my mother's face. Gradually after four or five minutes, the apparition faded, leaving my mother soothed and reassured. After a difficult surgery and a long recuperation, Robert did recover, and from that day forward my mother fervently believed in angels.

I have often had dreams that come true and I pay great attention to them, especially the dreams that occur from five to seven o'clock in the morning. This seems to be a time when our angels and spiritual guides like to converse with us, perhaps because we are just coming out of sleep and are in the right state of consciousness. It is a well-known fact that practitioners of Wicca keep a dream diary, which they call "The Book of Shadows." In this, they record their dreams and premonitions, dating them carefully. I have found with dream information that you may be given a dream that will occur in a few days' time, but also in the same dream, something that might happen that is two or three years in the future. This is why it is so important to write these dreams down and date them as soon as you can, and to note down as much detail as you can remember. One particular morning, I had a vivid and very disturbing dream.

An Angel of Death

In the dream, my spiritual guide appeared and took me into a special room where I waited nervously for someone very important to come; even my guide seemed to be on edge.

Suddenly I became aware of a very tall and overpowering being, staring right through me. He was dressed in a black frock coat with a snowy white cravat at his throat. His gaze was unrelenting; he seemed to have locked minds with me. Nonetheless, I was struck by how beautiful he was. He had thick dark hair, a long thin face, and liquid brown eyes; his arms were folded firmly over his chest. I knew instinctively that he was one of the Angels of Death and my next alarmed thought was, "Well this is it Beleta, it looks like you are going to die, girl, and he's here to take you home."

His eyes held great compassion and deep love, telling me not to worry, as it was someone else who was going to pass over soon. I heard his thoughts in my head as he asked me to help him with an important project concerning this person in the near future. He said I would need to be in contact with many people and he asked if I would mind doing this for him. I nodded my head in complete awe and wondered why he had come to asked me of all people, when there were far better folk out there in the world than little ole' me!

And then he smiled and I was dazzled. He informed me that if it were my time to go back into the spirit realms, his arms would have been wide open to welcome me. We both giggled, and I marveled at the discovery that angels have a great sense of humor— even the Angel of Death!

I awoke with a start and wondered if I had really been communicating with an Angel of Death, or was my mother right when she often remarked to me as a little girl, "Child, you've really got far too much imagination!" If the dream was correct, then what exactly did the angel want me to do and, worst still, who was going to die?

Through extensive reading and doing angelic research, I had believed Metatron to be the prime Angel of Death, but this dream told me otherwise. There were numerous angels who were in service for this particular task. Many, for instance, would be needed when there were world disasters or war.

A few days later my doorbell rang and two of my clients, Alan and Shirley, who were husband and wife, asked if they could come in as they had some important news. I ushered them into the lounge and they immediately told me they had been to see one of my friends, Irena, who was a well-known and loved spiritual healer in the area. Their appointment with her had been scheduled for ten o'clock that morning, but they could not understand why she had not answered the doorbell. A next-door neighbor came out and told them that Irena had had a brain hemorrhage while driving her car the previous evening, and that she had died.

After my clients had gone, I sat in total shock. Irena had no close family in the area. Her son was away, and no one knew that she had died! As Irena and I moved in the same social circles, I sat by my phone and had the dreadful task of informing everyone (even her recently divorced ex-husband) with the sad news. After many telephone calls, I felt exhausted with the grief and tears of her friends and clients, to whom I was passing this sad news. Then I remembered the angel telling me I would have to contact many people for him. This sad atmosphere prevailed for some weeks afterward because Irena's clients, who understandably couldn't locate her, contacted me to ask for her telephone number.

When it came to the funeral, the crematorium was full, and I realized how this wonderful person had touched the lives of so many others and how she had given help and love to each and every one of them. It was only then I knew how special she was to the spirit world too, especially the angel who had come to tell me of her death.

Through this experience I know every little kindness we give to others is noted. From it, we gain unconditional love and thanks from the angelic realms. I also become aware of the prior knowledge that these beings have of our deaths, and the deaths of every creature. It would seem that we can't hide anything from them.

Dream Work

Angels will cheer you up if you are at your wits' end and they will connect with you, especially in dreams, and they will encourage you toward dream work. Our days are far too busy to find time for total peace and relaxation. Noise pollution is a major factor in stopping us from connecting to the Divine source. Our ancestors did not have this problem so much, since life was much simpler before cars, telephones, and televisions. Most of us live in a busy society and we are often ruled by the clock, so sometimes we forget to take the time to connect with our inner selves.

Only in sleep can we be our true selves and cast off the burdens of everyday life. Many people claim they never dream or they cannot remember their dreams, but we all dream and everything is embedded deeply in our subconscious. Our brain is like a sophisticated computer and we have to find the magic key to unlock all of the information that dwells within.

I remember clearly as a child wanting to go to bed early so that I could connect with these wonderful Beings and be reassured everything was okay. I loved art, and sometimes a creative angel would show me interesting color blends and patterns while I was asleep. I have always kept a "dream diary," and I have been amazed at how accurate some of the dreams are.

If you want to connect with the angelic vibration or your spiritual guide while you sleep, say a prayer beforehand for guidance and premonition in dream sleep. It is not rocket science, but it needs a little patience until you get it right. There will be times when you will be successful and others when nothing much happens. I am still not sure whether the angels have times when they will not link with us, or whether it is our own inability to reach them.

Islands in the Sky

One very vivid dream I had a few years ago has always stayed with me. Again I was taken to the spirit world and was asked by my spiritual guide to look up into the sky. There suspended high above us, was the most beautiful island in verdant shades of green, cream, and orange. Waterfalls tumbled down and rainbows enveloped the whole island. From this dream I was taught about the beauty of the spirit world and how unlike our planet it is. Angels tend to the perfection of this spirit realm, and they are constantly inventing new things to delight us for when we return home.

Last year I was browsing a fantasy art sight on the Internet and one of the artists had painted a beautiful island in the sky. Perhaps he had also been shown the vision of islands in the sky by his angel in dream sleep.

Meditation

To meditate and connect with an angel is a magical experience and with a little practice we can all achieve this connection. Never think they are too grand to come to you, as we are very precious to them. You are as important as the Queen, the President, the Pope, or any pop idol or movie star that is up on a pedestal.

Preparation

The first thing to do is to go to bed an hour earlier than usual; you don't want to be so worn out that you fall asleep the moment that your head hits the pillow. Before you go to bed, be sure to switch off your telephone, television, and radio; get rid of any other interruption that you think could occur. Get cats, dogs, and children out of the way if possible. If you have a noisy road outside, wear some comfortable earplugs. If your home is normally chaotic, then you might have to seek solace elsewhere, perhaps a quiet park or garden. If you really need help and cannot get the knack of meditation, then see a hynotherapist and ask for assistance in the process. Anyway, for the moment we will assume you are tucked up in bed and absolutely quiet with the curtains closed and no distractions!

Your Meditation

Get comfortable and lie on your back, with a pillow under your knees. If you have some beautiful soft music, then you can play this to help you relax. Remember though, at some point the music might stop and interrupt the flow, so put it on replay. Close your eyes and breath deeply for about two minutes. Concentrate on the sound of your breathing and start to bring air through your nose, drawing the breaths from your lower stomach into your chest fully and slowly. Repeat this over and over again. You will find that you will naturally lengthen the breathing pattern and get into your own rhythm. Let your mind wander, and just get used to what you are doing. You can remain in this state for about 20 minutes or longer if you want.

Focus on your third eye. (This is the place just above the bridge on your nose, in between your eyebrows.) As you continue to breathe deeply, visualize the area of the third eye as a dark television screen, spread across your forehead area. Gaze out of this as

far as you can. This will take practice and patience. Sometimes it may take you two or three attempts before you get it right. Ask your angel to connect with you. You might say something simple such as, "Angel, can we have a chat?"

In your mind, focus on a beautiful carved wooden door and approach it. Knock on the door and wait for it to open. As you continue your breathing, deepen it. You will see a golden light appear as the door opens a little. Push it open and step into the light. Have a good look around. You are in the most fabulous garden, with flowers that you have never seen before and colors that are more vivid and brilliant than any you have seen on earth. There are exotic birds and creatures, playing and darting around in the verdant grasses; waterfalls and lakes shimmering in the light. Slowly walk down the path to the lake and sit on a bench. The water lilies are huge and iridescent, the air fragrant, and multi-colored dragonflies zip across the surface of the water. Feel the breeze gently lift your hair from the nape of your neck.

When you feel ready and relaxed, invite your angel to join you on the bench.

Angels
in the
Modern
World

2

There are many contemporary ways by which we have come to know about angels on a day to day basis. If you are just starting out on the "angel path" and want to learn more, I suggest beginning with angel cards, angelic websites, and exploring angelic correspondences, such as through astrology. And of course, all around you is artwork depicting angels—in paintings, in churches, and in statuary. Become attuned to the angelic realm, and you will be more conscious of the angels in your life.

Angel Cards

Today there are many beautifully illustrated decks of angel cards that you can find online or in bookstores. They usually consist of forty to fifty cards depicting colorful illustrations of an angel on each one and a small saying or affirmation. I use these at the end of my readings for clients who are spiritual and who love angels. You can shuffle the deck and pick one card to help and guide you for your day ahead, and usually these picks are very accurate. Angel cards can also be used in altar-work where you select an angel card for the problem in hand. Place the card on the altar alongside crystals, flowers, and so on; this will give your prayer much more atmosphere and devotion. If you want to connect with a particular angel in dream work, you can place one of the cards under your pillow at night, or you might prefer to use one in your meditation.

Angelic Websites

There are numerous websites that are dedicated to angels, and a wealth of information is out there for those who care to look.

The websites connected to angel art are wonderful and all totally unique. When I have time, I like to look at the pictures. Today's artists seem to have a better understanding of the angel frequency and their esoteric grace. Some of the old style painters from centuries past did not exactly do these wonderful beings justice; so some of them are in fact downright clichéd! I find this particularly so with some of the paintings of Cherubs.

Angels of the Zodiac

Some of the most important angels can be linked to the signs of the zodiac. These angels are from the *Book of Hours*, a devotional book made popular in the Middle Ages. This list will give you a starting point to see which angelic characteristics relate to your astrological sun sign.

Aries:	Machidiel	Brings physical and mental stamina and courage.
Taurus:	Asmodel	This angel embodies the spirit of rebirth.
Gemini:	Ambriel	Helps us to develop and realize your inner potential.
Cancer:	Muriel	Helps us flourish and develop strength.
Leo:	Verchiel	Reminds us to take time for leisure and joy.
Virgo:	Hamaliel	The angel of perseverance.
Libra:	Uriel	The angel of salvation and inner reflection.
Scorpio:	Barbiel	Bestows clarity, honesty and objectivity.
Sagittarius:	Adnachiel	Urges us to acknowledge and appreciate others.
Capricorn:	Hanael	Reminds us to give thanks for our achievements and share our bounty with others.
Aquarius:	Gabriel	Teaches us to take stock of ourselves and our lives, helps us be patient and honest.
Pisces:	Barchiel	The angel of patience.

The Angel of the North

This gargantuan structure of an angel is located in the North of England, at the head of the Team Valley, near Gateshead. It took five months to construct and it was completed in February, 1998; it is the largest angel construction known in the world today. This imposing sculpture is by renowned artist, Anthony Gormley OBE. Many of his other creations can be seen in Australia, the United States, Japan, Norway, and Ireland.

The grassy hilltop that it stands upon represents a megalithic mound, and for 200 years since the 1720s, the ground beneath was mined for coal. Anthony Gormley remarked that the men of the north toiled beneath the surface in the darkness for so many years, so by creating his angel in the light, this was a celebration of their hard work and industry. The site was carefully chosen for the maximum impact. The angel stands 65 feet (20 meters) high, about the same as a five-story building, and the wingspan is 175 feet (54 meters) wide. This is nearly the same width as the wingspan of a large Boeing airplane. Each wing is reported to weigh almost 50 tons and the body perhaps 100 tons. The whole construction is of Cor-Ten steel and it has been made to last for a hundred years. Special ingredients were added to the steel to make it an interesting rusty copper color, and it can withstand squalls and gales of up to 100 miles an hour.

More than 90,000 people a day drive by this angel—33 million people a year. They marvel at its austerity and grandeur. Mysteriously, the angel has no facial features. Many have said that as the light and weather changes, they can perceive changes of expression on the angel's face, so this is truly a living sculpture.

The artist remarked that he wanted to create a feeling of alertness and space from his creation, as a focus for our hopes and fears. The angel is catalyst for gatherings on New Year's Eve, pre-wedding ceremonies, and also eclipses. It seems that this congregational site represents a link between the sky and the earth, to connect us with the unknown and the known, and to remind us of our own mortality.

Many have criticized the sculpture, especially the media, as being stark and ugly and the vast amount of money spent on it wasteful, especially since the bulk of the cash was from the English National Lottery. Others love its simplicity and think it beautiful. I believe in this secular era it has been brought in to being to remind us angels are here to stay, and perhaps because of it, a new consciousness will come into the world.

Some of my clients, who have been fortunate enough to see a real angel, have often remarked how large they are, often as tall as 30 to 50 feet. So it does not surprise me that Anthony Gormley has chosen to represent his steel angel in this way.

Angels in the Spiritual World

3

Wise men have said the angels of the Creator departed this earth after the fall of Atlantis, and because of that, human and angelic connection disappeared for many centuries. Other religions and faiths sprang up to take their place, and then humans suddenly realized how much they missed the presence of angels and longed once more for their wisdom and loving guidance. Many of us now sense that angels have returned en masse to teach and guide us to a higher consciousness. I feel that our acceptance of them dictates that we will soon have the ability to communicate much better with them. It does not matter what faith or religion you ascribe to; it is of little consequence to them. All they want is for humans to get back to the "Garden" and to the care of God.

Angel Music

One particular night before I went to bed, I felt very low. For the past six weeks, most of my clients were either suicidal or grieving for a dead child or spouse. I felt the weight of the world on my shoulders and I had had more than enough. Soon, I promised myself, I would start to look for another job, doing something more cheerful and less responsible. I might even be able to shed some of the extra pounds of fat I had accumulated over the years from sitting all day long, listening to other people's problems.

"My work is one long dirge," I moaned, as I pulled the duvet over my head and eventually fell into a grumpy sleep. As I am a very light sleeper, I remember most of what I dream. Straight away, as I drifted off, I felt my guide approach me.

"And what is this mood about, why are you sulking like a baby?" he said in a very matter of fact way.

"Life is full of doom and gloom, and I hear it all! Other people don't have to put up with all of this rubbish," I said, resentfully.

"But you chose this pathway before you reincarnated. You know you are in service!"

"Well, I must have been stark raving mad and I don't care what you think, I am going to get another job!"

He laughed good-naturedly and shook his head, "Oh dear! You are very willful, Beleta, but now come on, get out of this bad mood. I have something I want you to see."

Seconds later, we were on the peripheries of a spiritual realm that was truly beautiful. I knew from my guide not to move as parts of it were out of bounds to living humans. I could feel an invisible force field separating me from this angelic world. From out of nowhere, a haunting and ethereal music drifted over to us and I can honestly say I have never heard anything like it before or since. It seemed to be the music of all creation and all living things. As the notes reverberated, colors appeared in the atmo sphere above us. They were the most amazing hues that were definitely not of our world! I stood transfixed as I listened to the angelic choir and I felt their wings were oscillating in rhythm to the melodies. Music on the earth plane is nothing compared to this; how I wished I had a tape recorder with me! Each note reso- nated to everything that was good within me. It reminded me of who we really are: of our soul purpose in the divine plan, and the universal love, which is around all of us. I wanted to stay there forever, but I knew we had to leave. It was just a brief glimpse of a stunning angelic realm, and it was truly amazing. I felt so privileged and very chastened when I awoke the next morning and with renewed determination, I got ready for work with a much lighter heart.

Guides and angels have a profound understanding and never-ending patience, plus a strong sense of humor. They never tire of us because they know us, inside and out.

Angels or Guides?

As a clairvoyant, I am often asked the difference between spiritual guides and angels. The frequently asked question is, "Are they one and the same?" This is a common misconception. We have to consider that, unlike angels, guides in the past have lived on our planet and they have individual personalities. Having come up through the ranks they have evolve into special human beings.

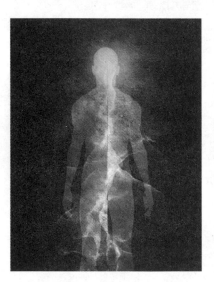

They have continued reincarnating until they have gained a form of perfection. The next step in their evolution is to become even more knowledgeable in the spirit world, and to dedicate themselves to helping humanity. In this way they can elevate themselves even higher on the ladder of awareness and become nearer to the Godhead. After a time, they will become Grand Masters and mix constantly with the angelic frequencies. Quite a few of my clients report that their guides are Indian, Chinese, Egyptian, and so on. I think the guides create an image of what they looked like in a previous earth life, because it makes it easier for the human brain to connect with a face and form, rather than that of an intangible entity.

Earth Avatars (Guides)

Selected guides will reincarnate in human form and devote themselves to a person with a particular problem. This is especially so if that person has tried in many past lives to get rid of a bad habit and has not succeeded. By helping the person to resolve it, the avatars get bonus points and reach a higher level of consciousness. These guides are called "Earth Avatars," and there are many on the planet as we speak.

What is My Guide's Name?

If you do a small meditation and ask your guide for his name before you sleep, you should have the answer when you wake up. Think of the first name that comes into your head and you will be more or less right. Sometimes your guides will give you special clues. You might hear a name on the radio two or three times in one day, and then again on the television in the evening. Perhaps you might be stuck behind a transport truck with the same name emblazoned across the rear of the vehicle or you might be introduced to someone with the exact title. It pays to be observant of the ways of the spiritual world. Angels delight in the synchronicity of three, and when that occurs, you can rely on the information. I am sure you have heard of the old saying "Everything happens in threes!"

How Many Guides Do We Have?

We may have two or three guides to aid us through the different stages of our life. "Why do we have guides when an angel will do?" I have often wondered this myself, but I believe the guides are dedicated to helping us with our day-to-day problems and they enjoy interacting with us, especially while we sleep, hence the old saying, "Go to bed with a worry and you will wake up with the answer."

Perhaps the guides are the primary school teachers and the angels are the senior teachers. Until we can advance spiritually, these loving beings can help bridge the gap for us until we are ready for communication with the angels.

Family Guides

In addition to guides, we often have family caring for us, after they have passed into the spirit world. A beloved husband might make his presence known by moving an object, or it may even get lost for a day or two, and then reappear in a most unlikely place.

A deceased mother might waft her perfume into the room to let us know she is there. When we think about lost loved ones, they immediately tune into us. Often a family member will intercede for us and ask favors of the spirit world to help us along our way. Our special person might get our attention by stopping a clock and then restarting it again. Family pets might seem preoccupied and unsettled when an imaginary "someone" is in the corner of the room. When this happens, we must try and focus on who has come to visit.

Animal Guides

Some religions believe animals have no soul and therefore cannot enter the Kingdom of Heaven. I find this concept appalling. How many of us have loved and mourned the loss of a pet who has been a best friend and confidante? Animals are very important to the angelic realms and as humans we have been given sovereignty over all creatures. Animals sacrifice themselves to become our food and clothing, asking little in return, except kind treatment and respect. Our pets love to be with us and to live as a part of the family. After all, a parrot will even learn to imitate our speech as a compliment and connection.

Where Do Animals Go When They Die?

When a creature passes into spirit it reunites with its collective vibration. For example, there is a feline vibration, a canine vibration, an avian vibration, a bovine and equine vibration and so on . . . a unique place where each species resides in perfect harmony. If they wish to connect with the other animal vibrations, they can do so, including the human vibration.

I believe there is a special plane for them, and once back in the spirit world we can visit them whenever we want. Angels dutifully minister to their needs. If a departed pet should want to come and visit you, it can do so, especially when it feels the need to bring comfort. It will often stay for quite a while and you might even catch a magical glimpse of a tail disappearing around the door. I could feel my Siamese cat, George, around me for about two years and then suddenly he disappeared. No doubt he is very now happy and preoccupied in his new spiritual home.

Once I remember awakening slowly from a morning dream in which I had been with my white miniature poodle that had died many years before at the grand age of 17. My eyes were still closed when I suddenly felt a warm bundle being put in my arms. I knew it was my dog. I dared not open my eyes but I cuddled her into me for a few precious moments. In real life she was a busy, wriggly dog that didn't like being held for long periods, but she stayed quiet and still, allowing me the privilege of her company. All too soon it was over and I felt her weight lighten and then disappear. Gradually I opened my eyes and looked down into my empty arms. I knew that she had asked to be with me, and that the angel of canines had permitted it. Once again I was reassured that all life goes on and that we will be with our loved ones and treasured pets after our time on earth.

There are many stories of near death experiences where people (and particularly children) are greeted by an angel who is often accompanied by a favorite and much-loved pet who has died. The pet comes along to comfort and reassure the visitor.

Power Animal Guides

These creatures dwell in a sacred and rarefied environment in the spirit world, but they can become attached to you. Power animal guides are mentally far superior to other creatures and they constantly mingle with the animal caring angels. Our own pets have to evolve when they die, so these fabulous creatures are icons for them to look up to and eventually strive to become. The power animal's role is to guide and protect us on our journey in life. Whatever strength or talent the creature embodies, it will gladly give to you. A wolf or meerkat will teach us how to react within a close-knit family group. A feline will inspire patience, psychic ability, and independence. A bird represents freedom and he will help you to lose your fear of heights. The horse teaches graceful movement and deportment. Are you clumsy in this life? If so, concentrate on the equine vibration. The fabulous unicorn will instruct you on perfect universal love, as he has no dark thoughts, only pure love. He will assist you in reaching a higher, purer vibration.

So! Are you attracted to wolves, panthers, or maybe an eagle? It might even be the unicorn! The animal you favor will be the one that guards you, and if you are in danger, you can ask for its assistance and protection at any time.

A Special Cat Called Merlin

About six years ago my husband and I gave a home to two elderly Seal Point Siamese cats. The previous owner had died and his relatives had placed the animals in a cat sanctuary. Strangely they had never been named, so they were known only as "the big one" and "the little one." We brought them home, where we had collars already made up for them with their new name tags. After two days, Merlin managed to open the screen door and flee into the fields at the back of our garden. I was horrified. There are hundreds of acres out there. As he had always been kept inside, I feared he had lost his hunting ability and would never survive in the open.

He was gone for over 28 days and my psychic ability showed me that his vital organs were breaking down. He did not know his new name, he did not know our location, or us, and worst of all, I could feel that he was starving. One particular day, I was in my beautiful conservatory looking anxiously across the garden and wishing he would come home. My heart was low, so I asked out loud, "Elvenia, angel of animals, please guide Merlin back to the garden." With a sigh I turned away and went into the bathroom to wash my hands and prepare for my next client.

When I went back into the conservatory, Merlin was standing in the middle of the garden, next to the old stone birdbath. I was shocked to see how quickly my request had been answered.

He was pitifully thin and obviously unwell as I gathered him up in my arms. The family said prayers; my young grandchildren concentrated on the angel of animals, lighting candles and asking the angel to help Merlin recover. One of my gentle friends,

Wendy, came and gave him healing. After three or four weeks, Merlin recovered and he now continues to be spoiled by all of us.

Angels

Angels of Karma

The karmic angels make sure our lessons are fair, and that we can cope with whatever we are given in life. At every stage in our life, they monitor us closely to access our successes and failures. There are some old sayings, which have great wisdom and truth, such as:

What you sow is what you reap

What goes around comes around

Be careful of who you step on when you are on your way up, you could meet them on the way down

The karmic laws are very strict, so we get away with nothing. There is always a payback for every negative action. A thought is a powerful living thing and it can cause good or evil, so we must be careful about the ideas that we have in our heads and upon whom we project them .

The way we have lived in previous lives bears some respon- sibility for who we are now and what we have today. The worst offenses a human can perpetrate are murder and cruelty to any living thing. Only the Divine Source has the right to end a life. The creatures of the planet have no negative karma. They are not try- ing to redress the balance.

Angels and Pain

Although some may find this a controversial subject, many spiritual people believe that before the soul incarnates, it agrees that the person should undergo pain and suffering, especially when he or she is young. Angels teach us that pain heals the negative vibration of humanity's evil deeds in previous lifetimes and that it creates a sort of cleansing.

An elderly relative of mine once remarked this might be the reason why childbirth is so painful. Every birthing mother is trying to heal the karmic debts of the past by taking on the excruciating pains of labor. A prime example of intense pain was Jesus Christ, who was brutally tortured and crucified and who then died in agony to save mankind from the sins of the world. Many say angels ministered to him throughout the crucifixion.

Angels and Suicide

The unfortunate souls who take their own lives are never punished. They receive deep love and understanding from the angelic realms when they return to the spirit world. Initially, the angels of karma will take them to a place of beauty and healing so they can be restored to full mental and physical health and balance. It is believed that anyone taking his or her life must reincarnate quite quickly to similar parents and family background as before, and the individual must face the same hurdles again. There is no way out, but we are told the angels never give us anything we cannot handle. Although angels are always sympathetic, suicide is severely frowned upon because of the havoc that is left

behind; this "offense" adds badly to
the soul's negative karma. Think of the
impact upon the living children, part-
ners, and parents who are left to pick
up the pieces. The grieving, sadness,
and tears that can last a lifetime has to
be considered, as well as the guilt that
the surviving loved ones must feel. They
ask questions like, "How could we have

helped them?" "Could it have been prevented?" "Was it my fault?"

We reincarnate to dispel negative karma, not to add to it!

If you feel you cannot cope with life, summon an angel to
give you the courage and optimism that will get you back on
track. If we could only see what was around the next corner, life
would not appear to be quite so bleak, and our hearts would be
braver. There is always a new day to look forward to and we must
approach life as an exciting but sometimes difficult journey. Greet
the day!

Guardian Angels

A guardian angel is a savior who will be present at the eleventh
hour. These angels come when a great danger is about to befall
us. If fate throws us into the path of disaster and we are in the
wrong place at the wrong time (and most importantly, if it is not
our time to die) they can, by the laws of the cosmos, intervene
and save us. The time we are born and the time we die is recorded

in the Akashic Records, which are in the spirit realms, so there are usually no mistakes. I have read many angel books where people have remarked about a last minute reprieve from some form of disaster and help was given in the most unexpected way. Here are two that I have personally heard of.

Amrik

At the age of 9, Amrik attended a school outing in the Malvern Hills in Worcester, England. The scenery was ruggedly beautiful and he was enjoying a quiet stroll among the grassy pathways, admiring the rolling hills and wild meadow flowers. Suddenly his foot slipped on a wet tuft of grass and he staggered forward. He was on a steep slope, so he couldn't stop and he started to lurch wildly down the hill, completely out of control. He knew there was a vertical drop of 160 feet just ahead of him and he panicked, trying frantically to stop himself.

Suddenly he felt a great calmness come over him, and an unseen hand pushed him to one side, breaking his fall. Lying on his back, astonished, he knew an angel had intervened and saved him. I asked him if this act of wonder had changed him in any way. Amrik said that his faith had been inspired and the incident had remained with him throughout his life.

The Boat

Ben is a really nice young man and he is very athletic. I had been doing readings for him for a couple of years and I always enjoyed his open mindedness. I once remarked while doing a palm reading for him that he had a strong mount of Neptune, which meant

that he should never drown. He breathed a great sigh of relief and said he had always been anxious about drowning. I tried to reassure him and said it was probably a past life thing.

A year or so went by and he returned for another look into the future. I informed him he was always protected in moments of danger. After the reading, he told me that recently he had been in great peril when he got out of his depth while swimming because he had a severe cramp and he couldn't move. All he could see was the water line in front of his eyes and he kept reassuring himself he would never drown.

Out of nowhere, a small boat drew up next to him. In it was a strangely beautiful young woman, who smiled serenely at him. He knew she was an angel. She never spoke one word to him, but she encouraged him to put his hand on the boat. She then led him safely to the shore. She disappeared instantly once his feet touched the sand!

Children's Angels

In Victorian society, it was well known that little children were under the protection and guardianship of special angels. Spiritually-minded people tend to follow this belief even now, and I feel in my heart this is true and it gives me much comfort. An angel who particularly loves children is Paige, so it is she who will minister to sick or unhappy children. If a request is made to an angel of children, the gift of a baby can be granted to couples that are finding it hard to conceive.

Adele and Mark

Adele and Mark have been clients of mine for many years. Adele emailed me one day and seemed very down because she and Mark had been trying unsuccessfully to have a baby for quite some time. After IVF treatments, nothing had happened and she was worried because her biological clock was running out.

"What can I do Beleta? Will you do me a reading and tell me if we are ever going to have this baby?" I thought about my reply to her for quite some time. Suddenly my guide's voice spoke to me, "Tell them to ask an angel." Immediately the angel Paige came into my head. She was, after all, the angel of children, so perhaps she would help Adele and Mark!

With fingers flying over the keyboard, I gave them an inspired reply. Firstly, I told them to find a flat surface and to put yellow flowers and a picture of a baby on it. I knew Adele loved crystals, so I asked her to place a piece of rose quartz with the other items, as well as a photograph of both of herself and Mark. They had to take a small yellow candle and inscribe on it with a pin, the words, "For us, a healthy baby soon."

I told them to light the candle and stand it at the front of their makeshift altar. Together they were to hold hands and speak aloud, with as much feeling as they could muster, and say three times, "Angel Paige, please grant us the privilege of a healthy new baby."

Two months went by and to be truthful I didn't give any thought to Adele and Mark because I was so busy. But then one day I opened my email and saw a message from Adele. I read it quickly and gasped. The email said, "Beleta, I am pregnant . . . it actually worked!"

After many years of waiting, their dreams had at last come true. Six months later Harry was born, hale and hearty, and the joy of his parents was complete. Many people have admired this little boy and remarked, "He's so beautiful and has the face of an angel."

Those, who are cynical might say that it was a coincidence. But I know in my heart Paige had really answered their prayers.

Leanna

Leanna Greenaway is the author of *Tarot Plain and Simple*, *Practical Spellcraft*, and *Wicca Plain and Simple*.." She is my daughter, and I feel, as every parent does . . . that she is special. From an early age, as young as 3 years old, she showed a remarkable spiritual side. To some extent over the years, she has educated her mother in holistic and esoteric matters, or perhaps reminded me of what I had long forgotten! I did not dwell on guides, angels, and life after death, or reincarnation, until I became her mother in my early twenties. Unfortunately, as a child, Leanna suffered intense ear infections and lived on antibiotics. She was forever at the doctor's office and seeing specialists, but they could do little to help in those days. One evening, when she was about 3 years old, I went to check on her, and found her sitting cross-legged on the bed. With eyes closed tightly, her little face was tilted upward in intense concentration. She looked so beautiful and ethereal, with her long dark brown hair tumbling over her shoulders that I did not want to disturb her. After a few moments, she opened her eyes and looked at me.

"What are you doing, why aren't you asleep?" I asked.

"My ears were hurting so much Mummy so I asked the angels to take the pain away."

"And did they?" I responded with surprise.

She nodded fervently. "Yes, pain all gone now."

Later when she was asleep, I thought about her words and wondered how she knew to ask an angel for help. I had never given any guidance about them; we were not even churchgoers.

Healing Angels

If we ask for assistance when a member of our family or one of our friends is not well, help will be given. Miracles can occur when a healing angel intervenes. The power of prayer is very potent, and it teaches us how to focus and draw the angels to us. It has been known after prayer, cancer will sometimes go into remission, and tumors will shrink and disappear, with the help of the Divine Being and the angels.

Angels
in Religion

4

Belief in angels is widespread in many cultures throughout the ages, and they are found in nearly every religion around the world. One of the most fascinating things is that accounts of angels are striking similar. This similarity is particularly evident when we consider the angels of the three Abrahamic religions—Islam, Judaism, and Christianity.

Islam

The religion of Islam ascribes great importance to the angels, who are known as mala'ika in Arabic. These are believed to be invisible entities created by the Divine Being to serve on important assignments. The most elevated is Jibra'il (Gabriel), traditionally known to be the mediator between God and the Prophet Mohammed, at the time when the Koran was first revealed to mankind.

The Koran says that each of us has two angels. One is a guardian and the other records our sins and achievements while we are on the earth.

The Four Major Islamic Angels

Jibra'il (Gabriel)

This archangel is the principal of angels and he communicates with all of the prophets in the Muslim religion. The Koran specifically mentions him and reveres him at the highest level.

Azra'il (Azrael)

Known as the Angel of Death, Azra'il and his helpers take charge of separating the soul from the human body before it enters the

ومنهم جبرائيل

The angel Jibra'il

spirit world. If you have had the misfortune of leading a dissolute life, then the soul will be extracted in the most horrendous way. However if you have led a blameless life, the soul will be taken in a gentle and caring manner.

Mika'il (Michael)

This angel is also mentioned in the Koran and he is responsible for bringing storms and thunder and lightening to our planet. His second title is the Angel of Reward, as he is in charge of meting out to us what we deserve and earn through merit.

Israfil (Raphael)

This angel is mentioned in the Koran as the angel who will blow the mighty trumpet on the Judgment Day to signal the end of the world. He is also known as the Master of Music and the Patron Saint of Travelers.

Lesser Islamic Angels

Munkar and Nakeer

These two angels examine the departed person's life and analyze his deeds while he is still in the grave.

Malik

Malik is responsible for the control and management of hell.

Ridwan

Ridwan is responsible for the management of paradise.

Judaism

The Jewish teachings on angels (Mal'ach or "messengers" as they are sometimes known) refer back to the first five books of the Torah in the Old Testament. Many stories are recorded of angelic intervention and help. In the book of Genesis, Jophiel cast Adam and Eve out of the Garden of Eden, and from that day forth, the cherubim guard the gates of Eden so no man can enter.

Many of the Jewish angels are similar to the Christian angels and they frequently hold the same names and titles. Some medieval Jewish scholars suggest that the role of the angels is

The angel Jophiel casting Adam and Eve out of the Garden of Eden, from the *Mála biblia z-kejpami* (Small Bible with pictures) of Péter Kollár, 1897.

necessary to execute issues that are beneath the dignity of the Divine Being, thus allowing Him a more distant approach. In the Old Testament, biblical angels fulfill a variety of roles, such as smiting the enemies of Israel, as well as the protection and shielding of mankind. Angels passed on information and messages from the Almighty, so fear and awe went hand in hand when these powerful mysterious creatures appeared.

Ezekiel's biblical description of these fabulous beings is truly awe-inspiring. "Creatures with four faces and animal countenances, wheels with eyes and four wings . . . and so on."

The Rabbis teach, "Whenever the angel appears, the Divine Presence appears too."

Michael, Uriel, Raphael, and Gabriel protect mankind during the sleeping hours, and the four angels, one at each corner of the bed, will ward off any evil. They can also be summoned to help a student learn and memorize the Torah.

All the angels of Judaism are male.

Christianity

There are many references to angelic beings in the scriptures, though there seems to be no specific dating as to when they were first created. Some say that they came into existence after God had completed his task of creating the earth. The Bible says that there are millions of angels whose role is ministering to mankind. The word "angel" comes from the Greek word *angelos*, meaning "messenger." The word angel is mentioned 108 times in the Old Testament and 165 times in the New Testament. All Christian angels reportedly are male, except for one (Zechariah 5:9). In Christianity, angels have no flesh or bones; they are beings of light and energy. Despite this, they can only be in one place at a time. The scriptures teach us that angels are not omniscient, but I am sure they know a lot more than we do!

A Selection of Angels in Christianity

Cassiel or Kafziel

This is an Angel of Temperance who can help with mind expansion and memory. He is said to be fond of dragons, but his main role is to watch over the planet Saturn. Also known as the Angel of Tears and Tribulations, he is the leader of the choir of angels known in the Bible as "the powers."

The angel Chamuel comforting Jesus in the Garden of Gethsemane, Carl Heinrich Bloch, 1873

Chamuel (He Who Seeks God)

This angel gave Christ strength in the garden of Gethsemane. He is renowned for his compassion and communication skills. He is said to inspire art and beauty and he is sometimes known as the Angel of Karma.

Gabriel (God Is My Strength)

This angel sits on the left hand side of the Creator and he is reported to be the second most elevated archangel. Some scholars say that Gabriel was female, and many artistic masters have created this image, especially as Gabriel is linked to pregnancy and fertility. He or she visited Zacharias and told him his wife Elizabeth was soon to have a child, John the Baptist (Luke 1:

The angel Gabriel of the Annunciation, 1501, Pinturicchio

11-20). The angel Gabriel also foretold the birth of Jesus Christ. Gabriel is thought to be a bringer of good news and in iconic paintings he is depicted blowing a large golden trumpet. Although he makes only four appearances in the Bible, the angel Gabriel is one of the best-known angels in Christianity.

Metatron

Metatron is the supreme Angel of Death, an enormous being of brilliant hues and light, the most elevated of all angels. He is said to be the king of the angels and he is often depicted with the scroll of knowledge in his outstretched hand. Thus he is known as the Scribe of God and the Angel of the Covenant. He was traditionally known as the prophet Enoch, who ascended into heaven and was transformed into the Angel of Fire, with 36 wings.

Sandalphon

Sadalphon is the mighty twin brother of Metatron and he is usually depicted as lofty and majestic. Attired in black from head to toe, he makes an imposing figure. His prime role is to fight the powers of Satan or the Prince of Darkness. Formerly known as the prophet Elias, he is summoned to help us gain spiritual knowledge. On a lighter note, he is the master of melodic tunes and lyrics. Perhaps he is in touch with the composers of our world and maybe he assists them with their work.

Michael (Angel of Protection)

Michael is one of the most popular and beloved of archangels because he is the angel of Protection and the celestial commander of God's army. He is shown with a mighty sword in his hand, ready to smite the enemy and wreak vengeance and destruction. He is often depicted in armor and he is beautiful to behold! He cast Satan out of heaven and he is known as "the Defender of the Faith." His job for the future is to weigh the souls of the dead on Judgment Day.

Raphael (God Has Healed)

This angel is the healer and protector of the innocent and the young. His eyes penetrate the entire universe and see all that is wrong. He misses nothing. Christians will evoke this angel for a miracle cure, especially at the eleventh hour. If someone in a family is suffering, he is the angel to call upon. He is often linked with

Michael, the Angel of Protection,
triuimphant over Lucifer

travel and safety. If you are feeling off color, Raphael will help: just ask him! He is one of my favorite angels.

Uriel (Fire of God)

Uriel has many titles: Angel of Music, Angel of Poetry and Verse, and the Angel of Psychic Vision and Nature. If requested, he will talk to you in dream sleep and help with any problems you may have. This beautiful angel will inspire art projects and psychic abilities.

Fire transforms and it is powerful, so Uriel is often depicted with a burning flame in his outstretched hand. He brings the flame of love to all mankind. Uriel was the angel messenger who gave Noah advice and warning about the great flood.

The angel Uriel, 1888, mosaic,
St .John's Church, Boreham, Wiltshire

Jophiel (Beauty of God)

Jophiel was the first angel to be mentioned in the Bible. His role is to guard the Tree of Life for the Creator. Grasping a fearsome, fiery sword, he had the awesome task of banishing Adam and Eve from the Garden of Eden and will deter any human from stepping onto the hallowed ground ever again. He has wisdom, will give inspiration, and help you to use discrimination.

Zadkiel (Righteousness of God)

Zadkiel is also known as Zachiel or Zidekiel, and is one of the seven archangels. Many pictures and paintings depict him with a small dirk or dagger in his hand. He is renowned for ruling over Jupiter and he guards this planet. Modern teachings lean toward him helping with our spiritual development and the power of prayer. This angel assists Michael as a sort of second lieutenant in battle.

Raguel (Friend of God)

Raguel is one of the seven archangels and he known as the Angel of Ice and Snow. It is said he will call forth the other angels on the Day of Judgment. In today's world, we would liken him to a barrister or a keeper of the law, bringing fairness to unjust circumstances. His main role is to keep the other angels in order. (Do they really need this?)

Hanial or Anael (Grace of God)

This angel holds the title of the Prince of the Angelic Orders or the Angel of Principalities and Virtues. As one of the seven archangels, he is honored and revered on the highest level. Some say this is an androgynous angel, neither male nor female and he (or she) will bring love and harmony to the home and sustain friendships. Dressed in colors of verdant green, with pale dove-gray wings and carrying a lantern to show us the way, this angel strikes an imposing figure.

The Angelic Hierachy

Throughout the ages, the church and scholars have come to the conclusion that angels are divided into different ranks or clans, and that they have individual duties to perform for mankind and the universe. No one is quite sure about how many orders exist— some say nine, others twelve.

The angelic choirs circling the abode of God, from Dante's *Paradiso*, illustrated by Gustave Doré.

The Nine Orders (or Choirs of Angels)

The Seraphim

The Cherubim

The Thrones

The Dominions

The Virtues

The Powers

The Principalities

The Archangels

The Angels

The seraphim, the cherubim, and the thrones, collectively, are the first triad or trinity of angels.

The Seraphim (Fire Maker or Fiery Serpents)

Seraphim are the highest angelic class and they serve as the care-takers of God's throne.

The leader of the seraphim is Uriel. The seraphim love music and they sing constantly. They are often depicted in iconic paintings and works of art with long golden trumpets, uplifted in worship of the Creator. These wonderful beings of such intense light and radi-ance often dazzle the lesser angels, who find it uncomfortable even to gaze at them. The seraphim regulate the heavenly movements and pass the light of the Divine to the lower ranks of angels and creatures of our world.

A 16th century depiction of the cherubim and chariot vision, based on the description by Ezekiel.

The Cherubim (Full of Knowledge)

Cherubim guard the way to the Tree of Life in the Garden of Eden and the throne of God.

The principle of the cherubim is Jophiel. These angels are the college students of the heavenly realms, and they have unlimited knowledge and divine wisdom. One of their main tasks is to make sure all universal laws are adhered to. Karma comes high on their list of priorities and any action that a human incurs or projects toward another will always have good or bad influences returned on them. The cherubim's judgment is fair and they inspire others to spiritual renewal and remind us of the laws of cause and effect.

The Thrones (Ophanim)

The Thrones, or elders, are living symbols of God's justice and authority.

The leader of the thrones is Japhkiel. The thrones are the peacemakers who deliver harmony to all negative situations. They can bridge gaps between the visible and invisible worlds, bringing spiritual perfection and divinity to the universe. They are impartial and strictly fair, but also humble in their service to human kind.

The dominion, the virtues, and the powers make up the second tier of the angelic realms.

The Dominions (Virtues, Powers)

The Dominions regulate the duties of lower angels. It is only with extreme rarity that the angelic lords make themselves physically known to humans.

The principle of the dominions is Zadkiel. This is the second triad of angels, and these work mainly in the spirit realms, seldom interfering with earthly matters. Sometimes they are referred to as "Flashing Swords." Their responsibility is for the universal laws to move in perfection and to unify and oversee the more junior angels.

The Virtues (sometimes known as The Brilliant Ones)

The Virtues are the ministries through which signs and miracles are made manifest in the world.

The leader of the Virtues is Haniel. The Virtues are radiant with resplendent colors that dazzle those that behold them. One of their many duties is to give courage and compassion to humans, sometimes giving a gentle push to get us up the hill. They are known to create miracles, so they are sometimes called the Bestowers. They keep an eye on nature, making sure the crops grow and that the weather is not too diverse or inclement.

The Powers (Lightning Swords)

The Powers are the bearers of conscience and the keepers of history. Completely loyal to the Divine Being, they are also the warrior angels. Their duty is to oversee the distribution of power among mankind.

The head of the powers is Raphael. These angels ward off evil or sinister spirits and they defend the unprotected. They will help to give you backbone and stick up for yourself in an argument or in situations of confrontation. They will protect and defend against anyone who tries to overthrow the universal laws and the divine plans.

The Principalities (Worldly Guides)

These are the angels that guide and protect nations. They are the educators and guardians of the realm of earth.

These angels have to set a good example to the lesser angels. You can think of them as the head boys and head girls of the angelic realms because their standards are very high. Their main task is to watch over our planet, it's people, towns and cities. These angels are multinational guardians of our globe. If you are unsure of where you are traveling to, or if you have a difficult journey and get lost, shout for these angels and they should get you to your destination without too much hassle. They have a strong humanitarian instinct and they understand us totally. They have a great sense of humor too!

The Seven Archangels (Celestial Envoys)

The Seven Archangels are said to be the guardian angels. They are:

Michael

Uriel

Gabriel

Metatron

Haniel

Auriel

Raziel

These seven emissaries have special prominence, and they are the better known of the angelic groups, as many people all over the world recognize their names. They have specific duties and assignments to help mankind toward a better understanding of life and values. Some are healers, others protectors and co-coordinators. The archangels concern themselves with the human world and they are here to be in service to us. They do not consider themselves any better than us, so if you do summon an angel of the universe, they must attend you by the laws of the cosmos. Each and every one of them has a guardianship role.

The Malakhim (Daily Angels)

The last group of angels are the malakhim—the "plain" angels. The lowest order of the angels, they are the most recognized, concerned with the daily affairs of living things. In this category are many different kinds of angels, with different functions. These angels are the messengers sent to humanity; your personal guardian angel comes from this group. We will focus on this group of angels in the next chapter.

Fallen Angels

I find it an incredible concept that a highly evolved angel could sin in any way, but yet religion teaches us that there are "fallen angels," or angels that have become arrogant and proud. The Scriptures wrote that the Creator had great compassion for them and that he would allow them to climb the ladder toward purity if they repent. In the teachings of the Bible they were sent to hell to mix with devils and demons in the underworld.

Daily
Angels

5

There are millions of angels that minister to the human race, and these are often called Daily Angels, and they can help with little tasks that seem complicated or annoying to us.

Not so long ago, a small wren flew into my conservatory and was crashing about among the flowers and plants. It was obvious she was petrified, and after fifteen minutes or so, totally exhausted. As I have two Siamese cats, I was anxious to make sure I rescued her, but she kept evading me and flopped behind the different flowerpots. In exasperation, I called out, "Angels, can you get this little bird out of here, please?" Within seconds, the wren flew straight down along the length of the conservatory and out through the doorway into the bright sunshine.

I often ask for help if I am doing a crossword puzzle and get stuck with the clues, or perhaps when needing a parking space, or even when trying to thread a needle. Angels love to be of assistance even in the smallest way, and nothing is too mundane for them. Why not experiment!

Angels of the Seasons

Spring

Raphael is known as a wonderful healer and he is the guardian of springtime. His job is to watch over the crops, tend the seeds and prepare the earth, especially if it has been ravaged by fire, flood or famine. He nurtures new growth and has strong associations with the Tree of Life. Sometimes if I have a sick houseplant, I will ask him to help it to return to health again.

Summer

Uriel helps to make the blossoms form, plants to burst into bloom and grain to swell. He is also the angel of music, song and karmic laws. As that old saying goes, "What you sow is what you will reap."

Autumn

Michael helps those who tend the land, such as farmers who grow and harvest barley and wheat, and who plough the fields ready for the winter wheat. He is the angel of gardeners and he gives strength and stamina for physical labor and toil. As a harvest angel, country folk hold him in high esteem.

Winter

Gabriel is connected with the wintertime and he helps to heal and nurture the ground before the next new upsurge of growth in the springtime. He brings harmony, balance and good news for a productive outcome when he is summoned. He is also known as the angel of hope.

Shape-Changing Angels

Angels can alter their shape and appearance in the blink of an eye. They can be huge and fill a skyline or small enough to fit in the palm of a hand. As they are in every country in the world, and their appearance and nationality will blend with the type of people that they meet in the various countries that they find themselves. All angels are beatific to behold, but they can sometimes take on the guise of ordinary human beings who might be sitting next to us on a train or a bus. Children's angels will ensure that they don't look threatening, so they can appear as little ones themselves. They reassure and soothe youngsters, often leading them out of danger. Angels can also create images of themselves in wallpaper, fabrics, mists or clouds. Everything is possible: they really are among us!

Justin

Twenty-year-old Justin was in a bar having a drink with one of his friends. His friend had just gone to the rest room, and Justine was looking forward to meeting up with some other friends later that evening. As he quietly sipped his beer, an unknown assailant came from nowhere and in an unprovoked attack punched Justin's glass straight into his face. The shards of glass embedded into his skin and blood spurted everywhere as the man ran off. Later that night after returning from the hospital, Justin looked down at his blue and white checked shirt. Exactly over his heart area was a bloodstain that made a perfect image of a small angel. Although the attack was very distressing, Justin realized it could have been so much worse if he had not had the protection of his special angel. He has kept the shirt as a reminder of the episode.

Angel Feathers

These are the angel's "calling cards." Pay attention to feathers that you come upon, for these are often blessings—or warnings—from the angels.

Some would say my family is very superstitious, especially about feathers, and I will personally hold my hand up to this. Feathers are from birds, and birds are messengers! The North American Indians used eagle feathers to adorn their headdresses and costumes, not to mention their dream catchers! If you see a particular white feather in your pathway, pick it up because it will be a message from the spirit world for you.

Here are two stories connected with feathers.

I am not a very good traveler and I worry about getting on planes, preferring to have one foot on the ground. Each time I travel, I wait for a white feather to appear from the angels to tell me that I will be safe, and usually, one makes an appearance! I remember before a trip to Russia, seeing a small white feather lying on the Chinese carpet in my lounge. It had not been there the night before, so how did it get there? On another occasion, we were in a lift in Chicago airport, prior to flying and there was one on the floor right in front of our eyes. Coincidence? I think not!

Before another trip, when my husband and I were due to fly to Austria, no white feathers had appeared, and I was getting really worried. What if we crashed going over the Austrian Alps? My partner, who is more down to earth than me, glared over his small round spectacles and told me to stop being a drama queen. "Do you want to ruin the holiday before we have even got there?" he remonstrated sternly.

The following day, I had just three readings to do. My last lady in was Patricia. As she sat down, she fumbled in her spacious handbag and handed me a long white envelope.

"These are for you Beleta. I found them by the river bank when I was out walking yesterday, I thought you might like them."

Inside were three perfect white swan's feathers. I could have kissed her! Needless to say, later on when I showed them to my husband, he raised his eyebrows and shook his head in wonderment.

On another occasion, we had saved for three years to visit the Canadian Rockies and to take an Alaskan Cruise. I was unsettled and strangely not looking forward to it. Nothing my husband or my family said could cheer me up. Four days to go and I still had not bothered to pack. My mood was so black I could not lift it. I asked my guide to inspire me or at least inform me of what was about to happen. But no information came and neither did any reassuring feathers. Then my husband came in beaming from the garden—he had a large tail feather in his hand. "Look! Your feather has appeared. It was on the conservatory doorstep, so now you can stop worrying and get your packing done."

It was a magpie's feather and very beautiful with its shimmering colors of blue and green. But my heart sank like a stone. This was even worse than I had first thought!

The day before we were to travel, the awful tragedy of the World Trade Center happened and Canadian air space was closed!

Now I knew why my mood had been so bleak, and why these dark feathers had been sent to me. We cancelled the trip. The angels had sent me a life-saving warning.

Baby Feathers

In my job, I meet many interesting people and one regular client, told me a fascinating story about her daughter. After Jenny's reading she told me her girl had suffered quite a few miscarriages and despaired of ever carrying a child to full term. One day, while on vacation, they were both lying on the beach sunning themselves in their bikinis. Her daughter, who was four months pregnant, turned to Jenny and said: "Mum do you think I will carry this child full term?" Out of nowhere, a little white feather drifted down and landed in the girl's naval. Jenny said she knew it was a message from the angels who were reassuring her daughter that the baby would be wonderful—and of course he was!

Modern
Angels

6

As I have mentioned in other chapters, there are thousands, if not millions, of angels in service to humankind. The religious or traditional angels will always have their place in our culture and beliefs, but we must also introduce a newer vibration of angels to help with the day-to-day problems that we encounter.

The information for the new angels presented in this chapter was channeled to me and to some of my soul sisters many years ago from the spirit world, and I am grateful they have given me the opportunity to share it with you.

This chapter will introduce you to the modern angels, and provide you with guidelines for calling upon them and working with them. You should perform a small ritual and use an angelic altar that you can set up for each angel. This is important and will help the prayer procedures. You may find that the altar ingredients will have to be adapted for different angels in order to personalize it more for your experience and your angel.

Why Does Ritual Work?

Nowadays, we seem to have lost the art of ritual, while our ancestors were wiser and more in tune with this important element. The traditional churches and religious sectors still practice this, but perhaps they also need to update it. Ritual teaches us to focus the mind on one thing and not to be distracted by everyday upsets in our lives. Angelic ritual is important, as these beings want your complete attention to be focused on what you are doing, so that you can make the communication and prayer work.

At times we are unaware that we practice rituals in many ways. On entering a church most of us will light a candle and say a prayer. Making a wish before we blow the candles out on a birth-day cake is another favorite. There are special rituals for weddings and christenings, for funerals and baptisms. Singing the school anthem is a form of ritual that creates a feeling of unity and cama-raderie, as does psalm singing and chanting in monasteries and convents. Even in this modern age, the crowd at a soccer match enacts male group bonding with chanting and singing—and inter-estingly some crowds sing what could be termed hymns.

Prayer

I feel that we are only visitors to this planet for a very short time before we go back to our true home in the spirit world. For some souls it can be hard to be here and at times it can be extremely lonely. The earth is used as a schoolroom and we progress more rapidly by coming here than we do by staying in the exquisite spiritual realms. By using prayer, we connect to those we have left behind, especially the Divine and our guides and angels. Prayer focuses the mind, raises our vibration and reminds us of who we really are and what our purpose is here. Through prayer we are, "phoning home" or reconnecting with our spiritual family who will keep us centered and on track, especially when we feel desolate and are suffering.

The Angelic Altar

It is best to be well prepared when you wish to connect with an angel, especially if you want to ask the angel to do you a favor. Try to have a small altar set up at all times if you can, and keep some of the ingredients listed below on hand. This will now be your sacred place that will allow you to focus on angelic connection, so please do not allow others to infringe upon this.

Your altar will fascinate your children so let them make a little one of their own (perhaps minus the candles and incense for safety).

Preparing Your Altar

- A small table or shelf, even the top of a chest of drawers will do
- A cloth in a soft pastel color
- Fresh or silk flowers
- Crystals
- Small thin pastel candles
- A picture of an angel
- Your picture
- Any white or pretty feathers you have found
- Incense
- A pair of Tibetan bells or small hand bell

Once these items have been arranged, light a stick of lavender incense and waft it over the altar and around the room, then return it to the altar in a secure holder. Take the bells and ring them three or four times in the air over the altar. Replace them on the altar. Close your eyes and ask aloud for the altar space to be made sacred and pure. Leave the room and close the door for at least an hour. When you return, all negative influences will be cleansed. You will immediately notice a different, lighter vibration in the room.

(Many high churches still swing incense around the interior of the church to cleanse it of negative vibrations, while church bells are used for calling the faithful to prayer.)

Angels and Candles

Throughout history, flame and fire have been revered, and ancient people worshipped and feared the sun. Without light, our world would be a bleak and dismal place, so people have always valued illumination. When we light a candle, it is a brand new light that imitates the light of the Creator. The spirit world is ablaze with color and luminosity, so it's not surprising that all the major religions use candles as a part of their rituals and beliefs. When one uses candles on an angelic altar, it enhances the prayer aspect and it makes the procedure unique to the person who is praying. Different colored candles and fragranced candles can also heighten the mood for special entreaties. It is a good idea to have a stock of various colored candles in the home if you become serious about angelic prayer. Keeping them in a special tin or box protects them from negative energies. Hand made candles are better than mass produced ones if you can get them.

Angels and Crystals

Crystals are magical minerals that have been a part of our planet from the beginning of time, and they hold many mysteries and the powers of healing. Therefore, if you want to pray to an angel of healing on behalf of a loved one, it would be best to place a

healing crystal on the altar, and a good choice would be an amethyst. If we feel unprotected or fearful of someone we could use
turquoise, as it wards off negative energy. If we feel lonely and
unloved, a citrine will rebalance us. It is often called "the cuddle
stone."

Whatever crystal you use does not have to be huge; a little
pebble shaped one will do just as well.

Before using a new crystal it would be best to cleanse it in
tepid salt water, dry it, and leave in the sunshine for a few hours
to cast off any negative vibrations.

Angel's Hair: Rutilated Quartz

Rutile quartz is the most abundant mineral on earth and it can be
found in America, Norway, Australia and Brazil. It is a type of titanium ore that occurs within granite rock and it has fine strands of
titanium needles embedded within it. When held to the light, the
pin-shaped inclusions look multidimensional and golden, hence
the name "angel's hair." People born under the sign of Gemini or
Taurus are attracted to this stone. There are other varieties of
rutilated quartz that have different colors of angel hair embedded
in them.

Rutile quartz can be used to connect with the angelic realms,
and its powerful amplifiers will release blocked energies in the
etheric and physical bodies. Many healers use this crystal to balance and align the chakras of the body. When working on a client,
they will use this crystal to cleanse the patient's aura of negativity.

Spiritually, angel's hair can promote the gift of channeling
and psychic abilities, thus enabling one to connect to a higher

consciousness, and to reach the angelic realms. This little treasure is a must for dream work and astral traveling, and it should be placed under your pillow at night; it should evoke powerful spiritual dreams. It will also help you to put anything painful that has happened in the past behind you and allow for a newer vibration to enter and start the healing process. I sometimes recommend this crystal to any of my clients who feel under psychic attack or who are experiencing a strange energy in the house that needs clearing. If a home is haunted or forlorn, rutilated quartz is a powerful aid that will lead a lost soul back into the spirit world, and usher in angelic care and protection.

If you are feeling depressed or exhausted, keep a piece of rutilated quartz in your pocket for a few days. If you are female, place a small piece of the quartz in your bra or as near to your heart chakra as possible. It is a great mineral for lifting the spirits and putting the spring back in your step. If we have a loved one who is under stress or unhappy, the gift of angel's hair should help to restore the balance.

I remember many years ago when a client gave me a small round cabochon of angel's hair. As she dropped it into my hand, I felt a tiny but significant electrical buzz in the middle of my palm. I knew it was powerful and I could not understand why I had not heard of it before. I wasted no time in researching rutile quartz in every crystal book I could lay my hands on. All those years ago we did not have the Internet to help us, so it took quite some time to gather the information. Ever since, it has been one of my favorite crystals, especially as it is linked to the angels!

Angels and Flowers

In the past, the messages of flowers were passed down from generation to generation, but sadly I feel we have lost this information. The Victorians knew a great deal about the subject. We can see this in Victorian drawings and romantic jewelry that contains hidden messages (violets for love; red roses for passion; lilies for sadness and funerals; lavender for peace and healing; and poppies for remembrance). And then there are shamrocks, heather, and four-leaf clovers for good luck and good fortune. The Chinese link chrysanthemums with funerals, so they would never make a gift of these flowers to someone unless of course there was a death in their family.

When using flowers on the angelic altar, you must put some thought into which flowers you are going to use. If your prayer is for a child, then primroses, daffodils, or yellow flowers should be used. If your partner is the focus of your attention for prayer, perhaps pink roses or violets. Silk flowers are acceptable if you cannot find the required fresh ones for your altar.

Angels and Feathers

Feathers have been mentioned before in this book and believers in angels know a white feather is a "calling card" from them or a gift. Placing them on the altar is a compliment to the angelic realms and shows deep respect and devotion. As feathers come from birds and birds are spiritual messengers, we look on our angels as divine messengers for us.

Angels and Incense

Incense is used as a purifier, especially in Asian countries. It cleanses the space we are working in. Each perfume creates its own mood to enhance the ritual of angelic prayer. If someone has been in your house that you do not particularly like, then light the incense and waft it around the room to get rid of their energy. Poppy or hydrangea incense is particularly useful for this, and it smells wonderful. Jasmine is powerful as it wards off negativity, and lavender incense is a good multipurpose scent that will help with most situations.

There is also an aroma over which you will have no control—a scent you cannot create. I wonder if any of you have ever experienced the aroma of angels? Mostly, this odd phenomenon occurs just after the death of a loved one. The place you are in fills with a sweet cloying perfume of flowers and it is unmistakably spiritual, as we do not have that variety of scent in our world. Angels create this to show the grieving family the deceased has arrived safely into the Garden of God.

Now the stage is set for you to work with the modern angels. Let's meet them!

Paige, the Angel of Children

Candle color:	yellow, blue, or pink
Crystal:	chalcedony, coral or topaz
Flower:	daisy or primrose
Herb:	clover
Incense:	jasmine
Prayer day:	Friday

Paige is the custodian of children, aged from birth to sixteen. She is one of the leading angels in the spirit realms whose sole vocation is to guide the younger generation forward safely in life. As parents we cannot always be with our children, so Paige will come if we need protection for them. When you invoke Paige, she can help in all sorts of ways.

Paige can help with:

- Sibling harmony
- Schoolwork
- Hobbies
- Success with exams
- Bullying
- Confidence
- Social skills and manners
- Difficult behavior
- Sleep problems / night waking
- Crying babies
- Eating disorders (food fads)

- Support with divorcing parents
- Prevention against pedophilia

Altar Accessories

- Blue or pink feathers
- Something personal that belongs to the child, such as clothing or favorite toys
- A lock of the child's hair
- A picture or photograph
- A milk tooth (if you have one to hand)
- A school report
- A piece of paper, with an example of their writing or artwork

Once the altar is set out in the way you are happy with, close your eyes and ask Paige to hear your particular request. Make sure you really mean it otherwise it will not work.

Elvenia, the Angel of Animals

Candle color: orange or white

Crystal: lazulite

Flower: pansy

Herb: vanilla

Incense: lavender

Prayer day: Saturday

Anyone who has owned a pet knows that each creature is totally unique, having his or her own personalities. Pets bring great joy to many, especially the lonely, the elderly and children.

Elvenia will help with.

- Barking dogs
- Snappy dogs
- Bad hygiene
- Lost animals
- Cruelty
- Sick or injured pets
- Patience
- Introducing new pets to established ones
- Prayers for the animals in the world
- Threatened species
- Thanking animals for food and clothing

Altar Accessories

- Place some of the animal's fur on your altar
- Their collar or lead
- A photograph, their brush or favorite toy

Summon Elvenia to help sick animals or ones that are trouble-some or those who have been brutalized by humans in the world. You might know of someone who has been ill-treating an animal, but you can do nothing personally to help. Evoke Elvenia through prayer to bring a better life to the unfortunate creature. If you have a pet that soils in your home Elvenia can redress the balance. If mankind realized that by loving and protecting the wildlife of our planet, the spiritual frequency of our world would move up a level.

Seth, the Angel of War and Strife

Candle color:	magenta or white
Crystal:	bloodstone
Flower:	red poppy
Herb:	columbine, yarrow
Incense:	rose, geranium
Prayer day:	Sunday

Most humans think of war and death with trepidation but remember there is a beautiful and compassionate angel called Seth, who when summoned will help to protect those in battle. If you have loved ones in the armed forces, warring families, unkind neighbors or if you live in a violent neighborhood, you can evoke Seth to alleviate the aggravations and bring back peace and harmony. He is especially helpful when domestic violence is terrorizing the home.

Seth will help with:

- War and fighting
- The armed forces
- The police force
- Controlling teenage gangs
- Violent behavior or bullying
- Cruelty
- Difficult neighbors
- Family feuds

Altar Accessories

- A white feather
- A picture of the person who needs to be protected
- An item belonging to them, for example a watch or a ring

Idalina, the Angel of Abundance

Candle color: green

Crystal: quartz

Flower: yellow poppy (papaver)

Herb: marjoram

Incense: honeysuckle

Prayer day: Monday

In life we will work to eat and survive. If you have a job that you are content with, that is fine, but many people are stuck in mundane employment and wish the hours away until we can go home. By calling upon Idalina to help, you could find a happier and more rewarding atmosphere within a work aspect, and hopefully a promotion or a new job will be on the horizon for you. It is no sin to want a little extra money for yourself and family. Although I am English with an American father, I sometimes feel the English frown upon the successful, so I am more inclined to believe the American philosophy, in that work and success bring well-deserved rewards. As long as you put in a good day's employment, enjoy the success. Spend a little. Save a little. Give away a little. Money after all is just energy, albeit a strange one.

Idalina will help with:

- A new job
- Success with self-employment
- Good work relationships
- Financial reward
- Promotions
- Working abroad

. *Altar Accessories*

- Place money on the altar, either coins or notes

Shianna, the Angel of Romantic Love

Candle color:	pink
Crystal:	aquamarine or rose quartz
Flower:	red roses, jasmine
Herb:	cumin
Incense:	jasmine
Prayer day:	Friday

Love definitely makes the world go around. Where would we be without it? How wonderful it is to have a romantic soul mate? But sadly, soul mates are not easily found. There are more divorces now than ever and each of us will have perhaps one or two failed marriages. Shianna, the angel of love and marriage will help through prayer to bring more understanding, love and balance to your relationship. If you wish to meet your special someone use Shianna to guide you toward them.

Shianna will help with:

- Choosing the right partner
- Happiness in marriage
- Blessing a wedding
- Attracting a partner
- Unrequited love
- Reconciliation in love
- Sexual harmony

Altar Accessories

- A red glass heart and red ribbons
- A picture of your beloved
- Wedding band

Althea, the Angel of Health and Healing

Candle color: lavender

Crystal: amethyst

Flower: lavender

Herb: chamomile

Incense: lavender

Prayer day: Thursday

We all get anxious and worry over the health of others and we feel frustrated when we can't help them. It could be that you are sick yourself, and that you can't get your energy back to how it used to be. If we are not healthy then obviously we cannot be truly happy. Our lives can seem tedious and dreary and often we end up depressed. Althea is the angel of healing and well being. Ask through prayer and she will create more harmony in this area.

ANGELS PLAIN AND SIMPLE

She will bring cures and hopefulness to improve the situation for us all.

Althea will help with:

- More energy
- Healing wounds
- Operations
- Dental
- Sick loved ones
- Mental illness
- Stamina
- Diet

Altar Accessories

- A picture of the sick person
- Something that belongs to them

Erin, the Angel of Peace

Candle color:	white
Crystal:	chalcedony
Flower:	lily
Herb:	hyacinth
Incense:	lavender
Prayer day:	Sunday

The world is a minefield of upset and unhappiness and most times we just worry and feels helpless, especially now that the television brings every part of the earth's problems into our lounge. Our ancestors only needed to fret about their village or town, but unfortunately we get to see most of the world's disasters, and it can be very depressing, especially to those who are sensitive. My Guide once said to me, "Keep your own home happy and your back yard tidy; if each and every one of you did this, the world would be a better place."

Erin will help with:

- World Peace
- Feeling safe
- Anxiety
- A good night's sleep

Altar Accessories

- A picture of a white dove

If we have no peace of mind and cannot settle, this can be very draining. Lying awake at night with our head churning over events that we cannot control can be soul destroying. Sleep is interrupted and nightmares ensue, leaving us tired and weary before we even set out on yet another day of worry. Angelic help is at hand and we can take the opportunity to grow calm and peaceful again with Erin. If we are given a problem there will always be a solution somewhere.

Gwendolyn, the Angel of Psychic Ability

Candle color: turquoise, purple or white

Crystal: lapis lazuli, moonstone, opal, tiger's eye

Flower: orchid

Herb: star anise, thyme

Incense: opium

Prayer day: Saturday

To grow psychically is the most wonderful thing to experience. Can you imagine looking at someone and sensing they are good or bad, or best of all, being able to take a peep into the future? What you cannot achieve in the daytime, you can when your mind is in a different consciousness, e.g. during dream sleep. Gwendolyn is one of the angels of dream-work and while you sleep, she will come and tell you what you need to know. Sleeping with a lapis lazuli or angel's hair crystal on the throat chakra can make our dreams incredibly revealing—with Gwendolyn's help.

Gwendolyn will help with:

- Psychic dreams
- Psychic development
- Communicating with loved ones in spirit
- Reading peoples mind
- Finding the truth in hidden situations

Altar Accessories

- Crystal ball

Jago, the Angel of Laughter and Fun

Candle color: pale green

Crystal: aventurine

Flower: buttercup

Herb: saffron

Incense: geranium

Prayer day: Saturday

Jago is the angel of fun and humor. Sometimes we need a good sense of humor to allow us to get through the grind of life. Laughter is healing and it brings friendship and optimism. It is far better to be happy than sad, so if your spirits are down and you see no joy in life, evoke the angel Jago to help uplift your hearts and see a more positive side to life. He works well when miserable or negative people who dampen your mood surround you. Ask him to cheer them up as well!

Jago will help to:

- Bring optimism
- Laughter and fun
- Enjoy and create parties
- Cheer up the sad
- Make others happy

Altar Accessories

- Picture of a clown

Benedict, the Angel of Meditation

Candle color:	lavender or white
Crystal:	moonstone, opal
Flower:	pansy
Herb:	lemon grass
Incense:	patchouli
Prayer day:	Thursday

Benedict, "Blessed by God," is the angel who aids meditation and mind focus. Fifteen minutes of meditation can be worth three hours' sleep, so it is essential to master the skill. Meditation will help you link with your guides and angels with more freedom. Consider that these wonderful beings are on the end of a telephone line, but you have to find their telephone number. With practice it can be done, especially with Benedict's help.

Benedict will help with:

- Getting back to sleep
- Calming your mind
- Clearer focus
- Connecting with your guides and angels
- Tranquility

Meditation is not easy because our minds wander and we dwell on worries of our busy day. Noise pollution distracts us as well. So how do we shut off and find some peace? Put in your earphones and listen to meditation music, go to bed early, and then evoke Benedict—he will help you achieve tranquility.

Zoe, the Angel of Pregnancy and Fertility

Candle color:	blue, pink
Crystal:	coral, hematite, topaz
Flower:	daisy, moss
Herb:	ivy
Incense:	nasturtium
Prayer day:	Wednesday

Zoe is the angel of pregnancy and fertility. If you or a loved one is longing for a child then ask her to help the pregnancy to come to fruition. She will also protect a woman who is carrying a child and guide her to a safe and happy delivery. If you are anxious about an expectant friend or a female in the family, she will listen to any requests for the safety of the birth for both mother and child.

Zoe will help with:

- Fertility
- Safe delivery
- Healthy baby
- Kind doctors and midwives
- Protection against postnatal depression

Altar Accessories

- Picture of a baby
- Blue or pink ribbons

If you are pregnant, ask Zoe to show you the baby's correct name during dream sleep. Have you ever met someone and felt his or her name was wrong? Obviously the mother did not heed the wisdom of Zoe before naming her offspring. The angel Paige can also be used for help with all things pertaining to pregnancy.

Galen, the Angel of Knowledge

Candle color:	blue
Crystal:	lace agate, pyrite
Flower:	chrysanthemum
Herb:	jasmine
Incense:	jasmine
Prayer day:	Friday

Knowledge comes from truth, wisdom, and vision. Galen is the angel of intelligence who encourages us to widen our horizons and grow through study. If you feel stuck and the soul is searching for more information, then evoke the angel Galen for assistance. He will help you to pass an exam, finish a degree, or pass the driving test. If you are a teacher who is unsure of your techniques and teaching skills, call upon him for help.

Galen will help with:

- Passing exams
- Driving tests
- New knowledge
- Teachers and teaching
- Invention
- Memory

Demetri, the Angel of Environment

Candle color: blue

Crystal: moss agate, pearl, emerald

Flower: sunflower

Herb: rosemary

Incense: dewberry

Prayer day: Monday

Demetri represents the angel for the country or state in which we reside. We all want to feel proud of our environment, so if you live in a dismal area that is ruled by low class people who bring graffiti, rubbish or disharmony, ask Demetri to restore the balance. Ask him to heighten the consciousness of others, to respect and love beauty. We can put in a request for him to change conditions that have been a problem in the past, such as flooding, drought or infertile soil areas. Sometimes a problem is deliberately set before us so we will practice the power of prayer to put it right. Use Demetri to achieve this.

Demetri will help with:

- Community projects
- Housing developments
- Parks, gardens
- Water and air pollution
- Flooding and drought
- Crime areas

Lillia, the Angel Messenger

Candle color: dark purple

Crystal: opal

Flower: cyanus, iris

Herb: yarrow

Incense: poppy

Prayer day: Tuesday

Sometimes when a great disaster is about to happen in the world, selected people will be given prior knowledge of this. It might come in a dream or through automatic writing, meditation, or a sketch that seems to have a mysterious hand guiding us to draw the picture. Nostradamus was well known for his prophesies and predictions. Quite a few people had prior knowledge in dream sleep of Princess Diana's death and some were told beforehand of the World Trade Center tragedy.

Lillia will help with:

- Informing you of world events and disasters
- Prophesies
- Warnings

My elderly gardener came to see me a week before the September 11th disaster. He showed me a small piece of paper on which he had sketched an image that his guide had given him in dream sleep. At the time it made no sense to me. The drawing contained two tall columns with fire spewing out of the roofs of the buildings.

Everything is known in the spirit world. There are no accidents whatsoever, so all is planned. When we have increased our spiritual vibration through meditation and angel counseling, we will be given these wonderful privileges. Lillia will guide us toward gaining prior knowledge.

Jarek, the Angel of Patience

Candle color: yellow

Crystal: aquamarine

Flower: alyssum

Herb: moonflower

Incense: lavender

Prayer day: Friday

How many times have we been impatient with others or ourselves? Perhaps a sick or time-consuming relative or a child is testing your patience and stealing the hours from your life. Or a work colleague might be slower than you, making you want to explode at any moment. You need to remember that your family, friends and work mates are all there for a reason, and if you have a flaw in your makeup, these people will expose it in your everyday life and inadvertently help you to correct it. We all find ourselves in situations that take us to the edge.

Jarek will help with:

- Finishing a project or task
- Patience with others
- Demanding people
- Irritating people
- Stuck in the waiting room syndrome

We must all learn to be patient with others and this can be achieved by evoking the angel, Jarek.

Zenia, the Angel of Friendship

Candle color:	white
Crystal:	bloodstone
Flower:	yellow rose
Herb:	ivy
Incense:	lemon
Prayer day:	Thursday

We all know how wonderful it is to have good friends, and some would say they are even better than family. As the old saying goes, "You can choose your friends but not your family." In your lifetime, you will only ever know a handful of the dearest people, some of them will come along when you are young, and others will become part of your life later on. You will click with some people, and even recognize them as a soul mate.

Making and keeping friends though is an art. You must never ignore them and always give them time if they are in situations of distress or illness.

Zenia will help with:

- Forming new friendships
- Patching up a row
- Helping friends
- Meeting up with old friends

If you are lonely and have few friends or cannot seem to keep them, Zenia will help to rectify this, or if you need new friends, she will bring the introductions into play. You might want to remain on friendly terms with an ex-partner in order to calm things down and to start the healing process. This is when her services are invaluable. Maybe you want someone else to find friends, such as a child or a member of the family. Perhaps you have a wonderful friend in the spirit world who is missed. Zenia will pass on any messages of love you want to give them.

One of the most distressing situations to occur is when rows and arguments have separated friendships. She can repair any rifts and help to patch things up. Make a request to Zenia and she will help with all things pertaining to friendship.

Pia, the Angel of Hope and Faith

Candle color:	lavender, purple
Crystal:	hematite
Flower:	marigold
Herb:	dill
Incense:	marigold
Prayer day:	Tuesday

Pia teaches us not to give in because she will find a solution to your problems. Keeping one's faith in life is important, and helping others to keep theirs is imperative. If your life seems hopeless and without happiness, this angel will bring the strength required to look ahead.

Pia will help:

- To restore your faith in someone
- To find a spiritual faith
- To find hope
- Bring optimism

Faith does not necessarily require a belief in a deity or in religion, but rather the knowledge that something better is ahead when our life is dismal or gray. If a loved one has gone missing, ask Pia to return them or give information to relieve the situation. Do not lose hope. Use her and remember that your lives can change in a day when you believe in angels!

Raoul, the Angel of Soul Mates

Candle color:	blue
Crystal:	rose quartz
Flower:	tea rose
Herb:	basil
Incense:	rose
Prayer day:	Wednesday

It is said that each one us has our own special soul mate that the Source has created for us. Imagine a circle cut down the middle in which one half is female the other half male. Eventually we go back to our "better half." If we are lucky we might be with our romantic soul mate in this lifetime, but it doesn't always happen, and many people spend their lives looking for this magical person to appear. I have often thought promiscuous types are actually searching for their beloved. When true soul mates unite, if one dies, the other usually departs shortly afterward. You will have many lives—a few with the beloved, but more without; if you were always with your soul mate, you would be too preoccupied with him or her and you would not attempt to learn from new relationships. United soul mates have been known to ignore their families, friends, and even their children in pursuit of their obsessive love for each other.

Raoul will help you to:

- Connect with a beloved
- Meet a beloved in dream sleep

- Get over the loss of a beloved
- Find a beloved

You also have family soul mates, which is why you may be fonder or closer to one child than the others. A sister or a brother could be a favorite, while you could actively dislike another sibling. We come from a karmic group, and in each life the roles can change. A son might become a brother, a sister becomes a friend, or a mother might be a daughter in the next life.

The primary soul mate or "beloved" is the most important and rarely does this role change. If you and your soul mate are both on the planet at the same time and cannot have each other, it can be a very tortuous life, filled with unrequited love, yearning and obsession. Have you known of a situation where someone cannot get over a love affair or the break up in a marriage? They carry that love to their deaths and beyond. Unrequited soul mates have been known to commit suicide if they cannot be together; a prime example of this was Shakespeare's Romeo and Juliet.

Raoul is the angel who will help you in soul mate matters. We might wish to meet our soul mate, or if the soul mate is not on the planet, we can request to be together on the astral plane in dream sleep. Sometimes the beloved will come when we are dreaming, and we may feel we have been cuddled or kissed, and we can often feel comforted.

Sofia, the Angel of Music and the Arts

Candle color: turquoise

Crystal: topaz

Flower: angelica

Herb: coriander

Incense: citrus

Prayer day: Tuesday

This beautiful angel will inspire and enhance your creative abilities or help a member of your family to do so. Children who are studying, singing, dancing or mastering musical instruments can be helped with her intervention. She can bring concentration and dexterity to little fingers and feet and young voices. Many people find her particularly helpful if exams are pending in the arts or drama. She will give confidence to the nerves of entertainers, ensuring that they give the best performance on the day.

Sofia will help to:

- Inspire in the arts
- Be creative with writing
- Compose music
- Give grace in dance
- Bring confidence in performance

Altar Accessories

- Crayons, paints

Ask Sofia to bless creative skills for art. If you paint and get stuck for new ideas, she will inspire with color and creativity. The same applies for sculpting, needlecraft, cake decorating, interior design, and decorating. In the spirit world, there are many angels who perform wonderful feats of art, generating beauty that we cannot comprehend or behold. We can be totally unique in our efforts and inspired with the help and guidance of the angel Sofia.

Dominic, the Angel of Mourning

Candle color: Deep purple

Crystal: Obsidian

Flower: Aloe

Herb: Calendula

Incense: Myrrh

Prayer day: Sunday

Dominic is a very special angel who has the responsibility for the departed soul. As the time for the person's death approaches, he will be nearby to lead them to the next stage. He will make sure their guide will be present to take them back into the spirit world where other angels of healing will rejuvenate the aura and restore the person to perfect health. Once this has been done, there will be great joy as the deceased family of the newly passed over person will be there to welcome them back into the family and karmic group.

Dominic will help to:

- Heal the grieving process
- Give strength when attending funerals
- Rejuvenate the departed soul

Dominic's other role is to give strength to the grieving families at the graveside in the months that follow. If there are mass deaths, such as in wars, earthquakes and disasters, many angels will attend the departing souls and ensure that they reach the right destination. Angels attend to every soul with minute detail and precision and there are no mistakes. The day we are born and the day we die is recorded in the Akheshic Records in the spiritual world. There is great order and no stone is left unturned. Dominic can reassure us on all levels of the death process and of the wonderful new life ahead.

Gillaine, the Angel of Cruelty and Revenge

Candle color: pink

Crystal: fluorite

Flower: lily

Herb: bergamot

Incense: lavender

Prayer day: any

This angel has a special role for those who lash out at others. Some seek to wreak revenge for deeds that have been done to them in the past.

Gillaine will help to:

- Abate cruelty
- Contain anger
- Bring self-control
- Control revenge

Altar Accessories

- A picture of dove (for peace)

Vendettas and plots can go on for many years and attach themselves to the families and clans concerned. Irrational behavior and brutality have followed us through every age of mankind and the strong have always persecuted the weak. Sometimes mental cruelty can be just as bad and can affect us throughout our lives.

Cruelty comes when an angry victim in turn perpetrates his own misplaced deeds on younger children or defenseless animals, and so the circle continues in its negativity. Gillaine is the angel to approach for these problems and with his help; many situations can be abated and changed forever. For every problem there is a special angel to deal with it.

The Angelic Garden

7

Some who are devoted to the angelic realms create a garden just for them, and they even put statues of angels around it. If you enjoy gardening, you might want to do the same.

Creating an Angelic Garden will provide you with herbs and flowers to use on your altars and in your rituals. And a lovely Angelic Garden will also serve to please the angels! Here are some recommendations for plantings, and where the species has "angel" in its name, I have listed those to get you started.

Angelica, the Herb of the Angels

Angelica is known as the root of the Holy Spirit and it is also known as wild celery and masterwort.

This plant is linked with the angelic realms; so many people use it for healing, health and nutrition. Angelica originated in Europe and Asia, and it is a member of the parsley family. There are over 50 varieties to choose from, and one that is really causing a great deal of interest in America is angelica sinensis, which is grown in Asia. Its properties are said to regenerate the blood cells and regulate the body rhythms. The plant is sweetly aromatic. It grows to a height of up to eight feet tall or just over two and a half meters.

If you really want to feel connected to the angel vibration, this bright green plant will add a dramatic look to any garden, but it will need moist soil and a semi shade environment. The small oval seeds can be scattered and left for the angels to watch over or you can cultivate them in a greenhouse. It will most certainly create a fantastic backdrop to any other plants that you have in the garden. One has to bear in mind that it is a biennial and that it will only bloom every two or maybe three years. The roots and seeds have been used for generations to flavor liqueurs such as gin, Benedictine, and absinthe. You can also grind the cooked or dried roots into a powder and then add it to cakes, biscuits and bread. But the most familiar known use of this magical plant  is in the stems of the angelica, which are colored and sweetened to use in cakes and cake decoration.

Medicinal Uses

- Respiratory ailments
- Allergies
- Anti-inflammatory
- Lowering a fever
- Digestive problems
- Premenstrual upsets and hot flushes
- A cure for flatulence and trapped wind
- Stomach cramps
- Promotes the regeneration of red blood cells

Angelica Aromatherapy

A lovely way to relax is to sink into angelica scented bath water. Just add a few drops of the essential oil to your tub and do a meditation to connect with your angel. Another way to chill out and dispel fatigue and anxiety is to consult an aromatherapist and ask for a massage treatment, using a blend of angelica and lavender oils.

Take Care

Angelica roots are highly poisonous when fresh, but once dried or cooked they are then deemed safe. Expectant mothers, diabetics and those suffering with heart ailments must not take angelica internally. If you wish to find and pick wild angelica, take care, as water hemlock looks almost identical and that is extremely toxic. If you ingest any plant by mistake, you must get to a doctor... and quickly!

The Fable of Angelica

We cannot be certain of the origins of this story, but the tale has come down to us through the generations. The story says that in the 17th century, a monk communicated with an angel in a dream. The angel showed him a magical plant that looked like celery and said the plant would cure the bubonic plague. The angel said it would also heal other ailments, but it would have to be treated with great respect. The wise monk acted upon the angelic information and boiled the roots with treacle and nutmeg spice, blending them all together into a brew of tea. He then named the plant angelica after the angel. This is where the story gets a bit thin, because no one seems to know the final outcome. We assume that it helped, and that the angel's information ensured that many people were healed.

Although that particular plague passed, the bubonic plague has not died out. It occasionally breaks out in South East Asia.

Mint

Mint is one of the most favorite plants of the angels. Apparently the angels love the smell of this pungent herb and it is supposed to attract their frequency to the areas where it is grown. There are quite a few varieties of mint and they are all appreciated. I suppose one should also mention catmint as this brings peace and cheerfulness to our feline friends.

Angel Roses

If you thinking of a rose garden then maybe you might consider some of these striking blooms:

- Golden angel
- Silver angel
- Snow angel
- Los Angeles Frost
- Beautiful angels

Iris

Iris is a beautiful flowering plant that should also be considered for inclusion in your Angelic Garden.

- Angel Chiffon
- Angel Echo
- Angel Heart
- Angel Symphony

Angel Plants

Plants suitable for an all-angelic garden include:

- Angel's Breath (Yarrow)
- Angel's Trumpet (Datura)
- Angel's Wing (Begonia)
- Blue Angel (Hosta)
- Guardian Angel (Hosta)

Angel Trees

Including a tree or two is a wonderful way to anchor your garden. Consider using these varieties:

- Angel's Tree (Telegraph Plant)
- Angel (Horse Radish Tree)
- Angelica

If you are really serious about your Angel Garden you might want to research the many other plants with angel in the name. A good friend of mine who is passionate about gardening told me there are over two hundred and fifty species. Happy hunting!

Angelic
Connections

8

A ngels appear in our lives in many different ways, and have connections with many traditions and professions, particularly the healing professions. Here is a sampling of some angelic connections.

Angelic Wicca

In the past, the gods and goddesses have been connected to paganism and wicca, and many traditional witches still prefer this form of worship. However, there is a modern take on the old ways that we call Angelic Wicca. This is a gentle and spiritual faith, that is used for healing and other good causes. One might choose to be a solitary witch or to join a coven with like-minded individuals. Modern-day witches evoke angels when spell casting, and use different angels for different situations.

A coven is a form of church or spiritual gathering, and just as Christians pray to the angels, so does the wiccan witch. Coven witches will send prayers to specific angels at certain phases of the moon, because when they work as a group, their powers are amplified to achieve a better result. If one of the members of the coven has a relative who is sick, a message will be sent out to the other witches for help. The group will act as a family of like-minded soul-sisters or soul-brothers, working together to solve a variety of problems, and the bonds formed within such a coven are strong and enduring. Many wiccans believe they cannot choose their blood family; so angelic witches believe their coven is their family.

Angels and Coincidence

Angels seem to favor the synchronicity of three. If asking for a favor from them in meditation or prayer, it can be helpful to repeat it three times to give the request more clout. They will often make things happen in threes to let us know we are on the right track in our lives. They are extremely playful and fun loving, so they will create small miracles that we see as coincidences.

I remember earlier on when I was writing this book and had just started to pen a certain word, at that exact moment on the radio the announcer said it. This has happened so many times since then that I have lost count. I am sure it is not coincidental. At other times a pop song with angel in the title would be sung on the radio when I was typing. As I said earlier in this book, angel messages are very subtle and there is always that question mark: Did I imagine that? Did they really do that for me?

Angels and Hypnotherapy

Some of us find it very hard to meditate and connect with an angel or guide. We might be easily distracted or the mind will wander off to more mundane things. In this case, hypnotherapy can be helpful, especially if we find a hypnotherapist who is sensitive and sympathetic to angelic work. My husband is a clinical hypnotherapist, and has taken me on many journeys, where I have been able to connect with my angel and guides. One might say, "Why do this when you can meditate instead?" I tried it purely as an experiment and I found it very helpful.

Some of my husband's clients have asked specifically to be hypnotized to the point of their last death and then beyond that. Then they have met their guides and angels who have taken them back to greet their families and their karmic group. My daughter did this and she was amazed at how many of her karmic group she had forgotten! To be fair, she was a little unsettled for a few days after the session, because she felt a strong sense of sadness and she yearned to be back with them. If you do decide to try this, remember it is not for the faint-hearted, so be sure that your character is strong enough to take it. It can be hard to live in two worlds!

Some wannabe hypnotherapists take a weekend's course and then profess to be highly qualified. The person you use should have studied at least two to three years before you can feel confident with them, so check their credentials to be on the safe side.

Dynamic Angel Healing

When a person is very depressed and holds sadness within themselves that they cannot seem to shift, an angel will often intervene to redress the balance. I have heard many stories of this sort of vibrational healing, and I have experienced it once or twice myself. The healing will usually happen in the early hours of the morning when one is asleep. It is quite hard to explain this phenomenon but I will give it my best shot.

One feels in a trance-like state and then suddenly an energy field of pure white light is forced into the solar plexus, then one feels as though one is being lifted off the bed. An electrical energy or a buzzy current runs up and down the body for a minute or so. Sometimes the noise of electrical crackling is heard. At this stage the person is probably semi conscious and he or she could open their eyes if they wanted to, but it is best to go with it and not be afraid. Afterward, feelings of floating or suspension will prevail for about five minutes or so . . . and then, sleep comes again. When one wakes up the next morning, all sadness will have disappeared and the body will be refreshed and energized.

I am sure there is some so-called expert out there who will give you a perfectly good scientific explanation for this phenomenon, but I know in my heart that my experience was angelic healing.

The Church of St Raphael

Recently my husband and I decided to take a drive on Dartmoor, which is in the southern part of England, in county Devon.

It was a beautiful February day, slightly overcast but with rays of sunshine casting little rainbows in the sky. As we meandered along, we admired the swollen gray rivers and fast running streams crashing against the granite rocks. The wild ponies and sheep were intent on grazing the short-cropped grasses on the moorland hills and they appeared contented and fat. Casually I remarked to my husband that we were in the vicinity of a church that a friend had told me about. It was called St. Raphael's and it had been built in 1869. Without much difficulty we managed to locate the little chapel that overlooked a winding silver river. Around the building were thousands of pure white snowdrops forming a pathway to the church and its perimeters. Outside, propped against the gate was a hand written notice, which said, "Please come in and view our snowdrops." My husband John said, "Well, shall we go in?" I sighed, "It will be locked. Churches today are always locked." Not to be thwarted, he opened the latched double wooden gates and grabbed my hand. "Come on, let's at least have a look." He pushed the arched blue door open and we stepped tentatively inside the tiny church. There was a hushed stillness as we looked around, and strangely, I felt the chapel was inspecting us. Sitting down on one of the ancient wooden pews I looked above the simple altar at a stained glass window of the angel, Raphael, resplendent in colors of magenta, amber and indigo. For a few months, I had not been well and had spent time in doctors' surgeries and hospitals. I closed my eyes and for some reason felt a sad lump come into my throat. I wondered if Raphael would heal me as I had come to his very special place? Silently, I worded a small prayer and asked him to cleanse me of any illness.

We left the church and strolled around the grounds, feasting our eyes on the carpet of snowdrops. On the journey home we were both lost in our own thoughts, when my husband turned to me and said quietly, "You know you've been given healing in the church today, don't you?" I nodded as I watched the grassy banks whiz by in a green blur and was amazed that he had linked into the situation. A few days later I felt better than I had for a couple of years and I thanked Raphael for his loving care in the simple little church on Dartmoor.

Angels of Disasters

The angels of disasters have prior knowledge of all the catastrophes on earth, and no one is overlooked when help is needed. Each and every one of us will be watched with close attention and devotional love. Some of us will have to die courageously, whilst others will live to see another day. There are no mistakes as to who goes or who stays in the Divine plan.

Often these terrible events occur to make human beings value life and to make us form a stronger community spirit. After all, we are all brothers and sisters. Out of grief and sadness comes wisdom and maturity. In the last two world wars the community spirit was notable, as others looked out for each family in their town or village. Today's society has lost this vital ingredient. Now, we are squirreled away in our own homes staring at computers or television screens. Our offspring are lost in their own world with imaginary people in computer games and DVDs, and some have little knowledge of family values. I must hold my own hand up and say I know very little of some of my neighbors, not even their names! Sixty years ago this would have been unthinkable!

When tragedy strikes, everything becomes real and we all start to pull together. Disasters can show the courage or the cowardice within our souls. A timid person might suddenly save another's life while a so-called hero will turn and run to save his own skin. If we speak to any person who has come face to face with death, they will always say it has made them a better and more knowledgeable person. If we decide to give our life to save another in a horrific moment, the rewards on returning to the spirit world are incredible.

Angels take pride in our feats, especially if we have valued someone else's life above our own. These beings watch every person closely and they note well, those who need to be tested in a dangerous situation.

Alcohol and Angels

Alcohol relieves stress and it is used by most of the inhabitants of the world when they want to unwind. I enjoy a nice glass of red wine, and it brightens up any social occasion. Unfortunately, if we drink too much, it can stop our guides and angels from getting in touch with us, especially during dream sleep. Heavy drinking in the evening makes a person more or less pass out when going to bed and will often lead one open to psychic attack because they are literally "out of it." Bad dreams or nightmares ensue, and interrupted sleep spoils the natural rhythm of the body. Care must be taken with alcohol as too much is frowned upon by the angelic realms.

A Brother of the White Eagle Lodge once told me, our angels like "clean vessels" to work with and drinking would inevitably block any connections with them. This also covers people who take drugs to escape the life learning processes that the Creator has put in place for them. We are never given anything we cannot handle, so fuzzing the mind or doping oneself to oblivion is just sticking our heads in the sand, and it will stop any karmic development. If we skip our lessons in this life, our next one will still have the same ingredients to deal with, but perhaps with no drugs or alcohol in sight! So in effect, there is no way out and we have just got to get on with it and face our trials and tribulations!

Angels
in the
Afterlife

9

I talked a little about the spirit world in earlier chapters, but I will return to the subject now. Many people who have had a near death experience talk of a beautiful white tunnel that pulls them upward, and strong feelings of peace and excitement on returning to the spirit world.

When we pass over, an angel or a guide will be present with us until we are safely there. Family members, who have previously died, will often meet the returning soul, and the joy is indescribable. When children die, a beloved pet will often be there to greet and comfort them. After the reunions, we are taken to a special place where the healing angels go into action to re-energize the aura and cleanse any sadness and pain from the returning soul. There are special temples and rooms of exquisite light and rarefied atmospheres where this healing process is undertaken. A long deep sleep will refresh the person, who will awake later with no ill effects from their previous life and with renewed zest for their new life ahead.

The Angels of Judgment

The next process is the judgment. This is not to be feared, as the angels of judgment are very gentle and understanding. They will never reprimand or chastise us for any wrong done in our previous life. Their frequency is unconditional love. We might have killed our own grandmother but that will not faze them. Their job is to take us to a special place where we will be shown a sort of video of our life. The viewing starts from being a child and follows through to our last moments. All we have obtained is shown and any negative actions are shown, without censorship. We then judge ourselves for each second of our life on earth. We see what we achieved and note the opportunities we might have lost, and we see how our behavior has affected others. No stone is left unturned, so it is quite moving and powerful stuff.

If we are truly remorseful for any harm done, we are immediately forgiven and the slate is wiped clean on that issue. If unrepentant, then we will have to face the troublesome issue in another lifetime. After the judgment the angels will ask why we handled a situation in a certain way and how we could have avoided it. Often, returning souls are shocked to discover that a thought is a living thing! We should never think of harming anyone, even though the deed might not actually have been done, that thought is still out there.

Angels of Apparel

Once the soul is judged, the Angels of Apparel show how we will appear to others. There are no secrets in the spirit world and we cannot hide our faults from anyone. Each soul has a vibration of light and color that surrounds it. This "garment" is a robe that represents the subject's true character and levels of failure and achievements. Within the colors, there are shades that depict each person's character, so if we were kind to animals that would be shown by one specific shade, while a bully would exhibit a different color. Collectively, the garment or robe could be stunning, beautiful, or utterly disappointing. Our soul groups are usually on the same wavelengths with the same shades, faults and attributes as ourselves.

As we progress and move up through the system, the story shown in the robe will improve. Sometimes a beloved soul mate that has moved on will stay and help the struggling person to step up the ladder and improve the colors. The Angels of Apparel are always present to encourage and inspire the souls to better themselves.

The colors of angel's robes are magnificent and beautiful. There are no blemishes or ugliness, just perfection, light and wonderment.

Angels of Reincarnation

After the soul has been in the spirit world for a while, it will be able to choose whether it returns to earth to gain more wisdom and perhaps to redress the wrongs that have been perpetrated in previous lives. Caring angels and guides will discuss what sort of life would be best, including the type of parents and siblings, the person's race, religion, cultural group, and the country they are to be born into. The "committee" even discusses the kind of a body the reincarnating soul will have. Many lives can be with the same group or family but roles can be reversed. A mother can become a sister, while a grandson could become a son and so on. If there was a bad issue with an individual in a past life, they will be asked to have another go at it, until the balance can be redressed.

We do not have to reincarnate but it helps us to move along quickly and to gain a deeper empathy with life and its problems. It would be sad to be left behind without our soul group, especially if they are succeeding in their own special development and moving away from us.

Walking with Angels

Nicki has been a friend of mine for many years. Nicki has dedicated herself to nursing and specialized in working with children. Others in her family have been connected with medicine, and her own husband is a very well loved and respected doctor.

About fifteen years ago, Nicki was in a phase where she felt like she had hit rock bottom, and she could not lose the depression that had descended upon her. One early spring morning, she decided to take a walk in a wood not far from where she lived. It was a quiet place that she had always loved, especially as there was a small, lively river running alongside it. As she walked along, she stared down disconsolately at her feet, trying hard not to give in to the depression that was gripping her. From out of nowhere, an invisible hand placed itself firmly on her chest, stopping her dead in her tracks. Suddenly four angels in iridescent white robes with golden wings encircled her; she was amazed at how tall they were, and she was struck by their androgynous beauty and long golden hair. Gently, their wings enfolded Nicki and lifted her higher and higher into a place of total love and peace. They told her this was the one and only true reality and she must not forget that, as all else was just an illusion.

Then they instructed her to look down into the wood. She saw herself as a little speck in her short blue coat amongst the bare trees and the little person that she saw appeared to be sad and helpless. The angels gave her healing, unconditional love and they lifted her spirits. Then with her eyes tightly closed she felt her feet connect with the ground on the woodland path. She longed to return to the angels and the place of tranquility that she had been so privileged to visit but knew she had to stay and continue to be of service to others in her job. After this connection with the angels, Nicki was totally revived and happy, and now if she goes through a bad patch, she remembers her encounter with the four wonderful angels and gains strength and fortitude.

Conclusion

If we take some time to dedicate ourselves to others in this lifetime, we become very precious to the angelic beings when we return to the spirit world. Teachers, vets, nurses, doctors, care workers, life coaches and any other job that improves the lives of others are valued by our angels. They give us rewards beyond imagination when we return to our true home, which is the spiritual world. We become closer to the Source or Creator.

We are only visitors to this planet, and this is our schoolroom of learning. What we sow is what we eventually reap.

May the angels in Heaven bless you and keep you safe for the rest of your journey on Earth.